D1488270

SCOTT FREE

SCOTT FREE

SCOTT ROSS with

JOHN and ELIZABETH SHERRILL

Illustrations by Linny Cobb

Published by
chosen books
Distributed by Fleming H. Revell Company
Old Tappan, New Jersey

Scripture quotations are from the King James Version of the Bible.

Library of Congress Cataloging in Publication Data

Ross, Scott, date
   Scott free.

    1. Ross, Scott, date   2. Conversion.
I. Sherrill, John L., joint author.
II. Sherrill, Elizabeth, joint author. III. Title.
BV4935.R595A34   248′.2′0924 [B]   76-808
ISBN 0-912376-15-5

SCOTT FREE

One night in 1969—it was early springtime—after signing off at the radio station and saying good night to the technical staff, I did not go straight home.

Instead I drove about ten miles out of town, leaving Ithaca's lights sparkling in the valley below. All over again I marveled at the beauty of this Finger Lake country in upstate New York. The moon was just past full, peepers were out by the thousands, fields were fresh plowed, or whatever you do to fields in the spring. I'd never spent any time around farms; microphones and turntables— that was my world.

And there it was, washed in moonlight, Peg Hardesty's barn.

It sat closer to the road than I remembered, right up against the highway, like most of the houses and barns up here where snow can pile up four, five feet. "You can always get your milk through a drift to the highway if you don't have to shovel too far," Peg had explained.

I couldn't imagine what had pulled me out to take a look at this place again. When I had seen it last it had seemed like a big nothing—just a tumble-down old barn like a hundred others around here. The silo roof was caved in, rusty sheets of galvanized iron creaking in the breeze. There was an incredible stink about the place, that Peg said were "normal" barn smells of manure and rotting straw. Maybe a little dirtier than most: Peg's husband was dead and help was hard to find.

Why was it then that I saw this old barn differently now, as I pulled the car quietly to a stop so as not to wake Peg in the farm house beyond. Why, as I switched off the headlights, did the place suddenly seem—I don't know. Holy.

It was more than just the magic of moonlight, which turned the old weathered wood silver. It was more than a night breeze which blew the barnyard smells away from me. I got out of the car and pushed the huge sliding doors open just a crack. Peg's dog Niki heard me and set up an hysterical yapping. Poor Peg—two o'clock in the morning!

It was dark in the big barn. Only a little moonlight came in through the holes in the roof. Off to one side I thought I could make out a pile of hay, to the other what looked like a vast junk heap. A huge centerpost grew out of the floor holding up the beams that in turn held up the roof. Somewhere in the shadows a cow heaved to her feet and stamped, waked up by that darn dog, no doubt.

And still I continued to look around with strangely opened eyes. Crazy ideas kept coming to my mind, like, with a shovel I could get the manure out of those cowstalls. Or, I could pile all those old boards into a corner.

But what for? What could anyone use an old barn for—especially me, of all people on earth? Now that my eyes were adjusting to the dark I could see that the shadow on my right was a junk pile, all right: ragged Sears-Roebuck catalogues, rusty farm machinery, an old mattress.

I shook my head to clear it of strange notions and walked out to the car. I intended to go back to Ithaca, to my wife Nedra and our baby daughter.

And yet I didn't go back. Instead I took a long rambling drive through the dark countryside. What was there about that old barn? It had a strange pull which I could not understand. Certainly there was nothing about a barn that meshed gear with our lives, lives which up until recently had been centered on the New York rock music scene: pot, LSD, heavy drinking, running around with the Beatles, the Stones, Bobby Dylan . . .

Where was that world now? Finished and done with in one sense. And yet in another sense filling my whole mind, just as bits and scraps of the past filled that old barn. All of us hang onto stuff from the past. Some of it salvageable and good. Some of it just lying there rotting.

Mine, my past, began in Glasgow, Scotland, where I was born—where the first thing I remember is the orange glow of bombs lighting up the sky, the shock of explosions shaking my room, my bed, everything . . .

2

I wasn't afraid of the bombs.

To me, night-time air raids over Glasgow were just the way life was—noisy, but not frightening. I accepted them the same way I accepted food shortages and soldiers in the streets, British and American uniforms side by side. At the first wail of the sirens I would climb into a chair beside the window to watch the city black out street by street, until all I could see was the flicker of flashlights as wardens went from house to house checking blackout curtains.

As far as I knew, life had never been any different. Soon my father would come into my room in the tiny walk-up apartment where he, Mum and I lived, and pick me up in his arms. Always it was the same. First I would. rub the end of his nose in a silly little game we'd somehow started. I rubbed it so often he had a shiny patch there. Then Dad would speak to God, asking Him whether we should go to the air raid shelter. I could never hear God's answer, but Dad could, because we hardly ever did go to the shelter. "We will trust God," Dad would say. Outside I could hear men shouting, fire fighting equipment rumbling by. Sometimes there would be earth-rocking explosions as bombs struck the Clyde Bank shipyards nearby.

11

I remember the first time I ever saw a frightened person—and there wasn't even a raid that night. Some people had come to see my parents, bringing a little boy about my age, three or four, I suppose, and the two of us were put down in my bed. When Mum had tucked us in, she switched off the light. Immediately the boy began to scream. His mother ran into the room crying:

"Don't do that! He can't sleep in the dark!"

It was my first encounter with fear. I remember feeling a morbid interest in it, as one might in a deformity.

For the most part this freedom from fear was an inheritance from my father. Dad was one of six sons of a small hotelkeeper in Inverness. All went off to the First World War; three came back. It was during this war, while he was in India, that Dad had a remarkable experience. He knew nothing at all about God when he left home for overseas duty. But one day in India while he was away from his unit, walking along a country road, a strange and mighty power swept him to his knees. He had no idea what was happening, except that he knew he had met God.

His conversion was as permanent as it was unexpected. But it was not something he could talk about with his family. He came back to Scotland to find that his widowed mother had nearly lost her mind with grief for her three dead sons. Soon she packed her bags and fled to America, where we heard from her only occasionally; bitter, complaining, unhappy letters.

Dad had wanted to become a preacher, but he had no money for theological school. So he became a mechanical engineer in the Glasgow shipyards, using engineering in the same way St. Paul used tentmaking; during the day he worked at the shipyards, at night and on weekends he lived his real life as a lay preacher in the Apostolic Church.

God was as much a part of normal life to me as the air raids. I remember sitting in the kitchen with my mother one day listening to a Bible story. All of a sudden, as she read, I noticed another person in the room. He was wearing a robe with all kinds of colors glinting from it like a rainbow. In his hands I saw blood-caked holes. He had no shoes on and his feet were hurt and torn too. I looked up at his face and had to shut my eyes; above his shoulders was a blinding light. I knew who he was and wasn't surprised to see him; what surprised me was that Mum just went on reading.

I nudged her. "Mum," I said, "it's Jesus."

Mother looked up, then around the room.

"No, right there. Over there!"

The person I was looking at was not a hazy vision but perfectly solid. Except for the light where I couldn't look, he seemed as flesh-and-blood as Mum. I jumped up and ran to him—and just as suddenly he was gone. I burst into tears.

Mother took me in her arms. "It's all right, Charlie. Don't cry. He's still here. Jesus is always here. Would you like to talk to Him?"

So right there in the kitchen we knelt down on the old linoleum floor, and Mother showed me how to say, "Jesus, thank You for being here. Please now come into my heart."

I loved Jesus, and I loved to walk beside my father Sunday mornings as he and his friends gathered a crowd for church. With a noisy, brassy band they'd parade through the steep, cobble-stoned streets of Glasgow till they had pied pipered a congregation right into their soot-blackened church.

But that was the only thing I liked about Sunday. Mostly it was a day when we couldn't do things. Other days, when Dad's shift was off at the shipyards, he'd take me riding on his bicycle—sometimes clear out to the sea. I could never understand why what was such fun on weekdays was a sin on Sunday.

Listening to the radio was a sin every day. The neighbors downstairs had a set but I was not allowed to visit them when it was playing. Motion pictures were even worse. Everyone who went to the movies was going to hell. So was everyone who smoked. This bothered me because I had a good friend who smoked. He was an American soldier who gave me chewing gum and I didn't like to think of him in everlasting damnation.

I was five when the war ended. There was still very little food and fuel but I didn't mind because I couldn't remember anything else. For a while I missed the friendly soldiers in the streets; then in the fall of 1945 I started school and made a lot of new friends. Now I hated Sundays worse than ever because that was the day the boys met to play soccer in a lot where a neighbor's home had been before it was hit by a buzz-bomb. Since it was Sunday I was not allowed to join them.

The real change in my life, however, the all-encompassing one, came just before my ninth birthday, when my father called me into the kitchen and announced that we were moving to America.

My reaction was panic. I didn't want to go anywhere. Especially not to America. America was where my angry, dour grandmother lived. And what about my friends?

"God is sending us, God will provide our every need," Dad said.

My friends thought otherwise. "Charlie will be scalped by the Indians!" they chanted. They warned me that lions would eat me and giraffes would step on me.

But worse than the threat of wild men and animals was the spectacle of our home breaking up before my eyes. Bit by bit, during that Christmas season of 1948, I watched it all go. There went the umbrella stand, there went Mum's kettle, and my little push-pedal car. The only things we kept were our clothes and some family photographs. Finally everything else was gone. We borrowed crates from the greengrocer to sit on. These bare, ugly rooms had been our home.

I remember a lot of people crying at the train station, then a long train ride. On January 1, 1949, we boarded the S.S. *America* in Southampton. Most of the passengers were still celebrating New Year's Eve and I stared at them in astonishment. The drunks who had sometimes stumbled into the church back in Glasgow were poor and dirty, but these boisterous, reeling people were better dressed than we were. Dad and I were put in one cabin with a lot of men, Mum in another with a group of women. The crossing was stormy all the way: one morning Dad and I were the only two passengers in the dining room.

Finally on the morning of January 6 we steamed into the Hudson

River. I couldn't believe the size of everything. Automobiles were enormous. Buildings towered higher than mountains. Bridges were longer than anything I had ever seen.

To make a good impression when we arrived at my grandmother's, I wore my best clothes, which of course meant kilts. It was a mistake. Even Grandmother, when at last we reached her house in New Jersey, scoffed at my old-country appearance, while the boys in the neighborhood were hysterical.

"What'cha got under there, Scotty?"

"Hey, Scott—can I have a date?"

I soon packed the kilts away, but I never got rid of the nickname. From then on only my family called me Charles.

While my father was trying to find work—post-war jobs were hard to come by and he was not a citizen—I did my best to adjust to this new land. First there was learning to think in dollars instead of pounds, shillings and pence. Harder to get used to was the amount of food Americans stuffed down their throats. In Glasgow adults drank ersatz coffee, kids drank powdered milk: one pint would last me four days. We didn't cut butter (and of course it wasn't really butter); we scraped it off the top of the bar to conserve it. Three powdered eggs would last the family a week. Here, two fresh eggs went onto the breakfast plate for each member of the family. It was incredible. The first time I bought a bottle of Seven Up I couldn't finish it: it was too much for me.

School was the toughest place. My accent kept the whole class roaring. The teacher was often angry at me for disrupting things, but I could never tell which remark would be taken funny. I remember the day I asked, "Would you pass the rrr-rubber?"

For some reason that broke everyone up.

"What's a rubber?" they said.

"I mean the rrr-rubber, the rrr-rubber you erase the blackboard with."

Also, at first, when the teacher called on me I would jump to my feet and say, "Yes, Miss," like we did in Scotland. She thought I was making fun of her and kept me after school several times until I learned not to do this.

I determined to become a regular Joe, and when the boys started playing baseball in the spring I put down as my position, "catcher." But I forgot that the bat is not swung like a cricket bat and stepped right into it. The next thing I remember is being carried off the field in the arms of the school sports hero, Manuel Simpson. Manuel came all the way to the hospital with me, and that made me a hero too. When I woke up from the anesthesia I had pieces of steel in my nose, a huge bandage around my head, and the news that I'd be breathing through my mouth for a year.

Perhaps if we'd been able to stay in one place for a while I could have earned my place in the group. But over the next several years Dad moved continually, from one temporary job to another —New Jersey, Virginia, Pennsylvania, Maryland—and I remained just enough "different" to be singled out as a target by the kids wherever we were. I was the foreigner. The odd-ball. The runt.

Whether it was the shortage of food my first few years or what, wherever we lived I was always the smallest kid in the class. Eventually I learned that my only chance in a fight was surprise. Once a kid walked up behind me and said,

"I'm going to beat you up, you little squirt, because I don't like the way you—"

I never learned what he didn't like. Before he had finished the sentence I had swung around and put my fist into his nose, hard. He doubled up, blood squirting between his fingers, and never came near me again.

In that same school another boy jumped me in the locker room. I twisted out of his grip, pulled his feet from under him and had my hands on his throat before he knew what was happening. The guy weighed fifty pounds more than I did, but it took two teachers to pull me off him.

Dad's income remained very low during all this period. Night watchman, chicken plucking, making broom handles—he never really found a good job. My sister Anne was born the first year we were in America, so now there were four of us to clothe and feed. But Dad never questioned God's will, never seemed to doubt that he had truly been sent to this "field." After work, every evening, he would preach—most of the time in homes and small storefront churches. Dad was preaching the Baptism in the Holy Spirit which was not widely accepted then. But he kept saying that he was seeing results. Maybe he was, but if the kind of people who came to his services were his results, I wanted no part of it.

I couldn't believe my ears as these loving Christians would gather on the sidewalk after church and cut each other to ribbons. As long as they were face to face it was "Brother this" and "Sister that"—but when the first one left! "I saw him on the bus and what do you think he was reading?" ". . . hasn't washed those curtains in over a year!"

They didn't carry on this way when Dad was in earshot. He hated gossip like nothing else in the world. But I might as well have been one of the neighborhood dogs for all the notice they took of me.

They were hypocrites too. I'd listen to them in church, Sunday after Sunday, "giving their testimony" about how they'd been delivered from nicotine—and know which ones had been sneaking cigarettes back of the building before the service. Just because I was young did they think I had no eyes or ears or any sense at all?

Sometimes I'd try to talk to Dad about these things, but he wouldn't listen to gossip from me, any more than from anyone else. He kept telling me I must try to see people as God saw them.

And then the thing happened which made me wonder if God saw anything at all. Dad had found work in a food-packing plant near the church where he was pastoring and since we stayed with a family who attended the church there was no rent to pay. I remember that I had my own room in those people's house, the nicest room I ever had. The man who owned the house said if I was a good boy he was going to give me a bicycle.

One afternoon I was lying on the bed reading, when this man walked in and shut the door. He said something about being tired and lay down beside me. After a while he began talking about my clothes—how they were too tight and he'd loosen them for me. I didn't know what was happening. For a while I was too frightened and confused to move. Then I bolted off the bed and ran down to the cellar and hid.

I was too ashamed to tell my father about it. But when it happened again and then a third time, I finally did. I don't know what happened between Dad and the man. I only know I came home from school one day to find Mum crying as she put our things in a suitcase. We left that same evening and nobody even came to say goodbye.

The funny thing was that outside of church, if only we stayed in one place long enough, I would meet great people. Down the street from our house in Winchester, Virginia, for example, was a little store owned by a man and his wife, Ted and Margie. They had a popcorn machine outside the store on the sidewalk. Inside were comic books, candy and a soda pop dispenser. Ted and Margie let me spend hours there, just hanging around. I was especially fascinated by the Wild West stuff for sale. By American standards I was too old to be playing cowboys, but in Glasgow I'd never had the chance.

Toward Christmas 1951, just after my twelfth birthday, they got in a new supply of guns and holsters. They were unbelievable. One set in particular haunted me. The guns had mother-of-pearl handles, the belt and holsters were jet black with silver studs. I'd go around whispering to myself, "Don't anyone buy them." I just wanted them to stay there where I could look at them. Then one day that set was gone. For days a lump came up in my throat whenever I thought of those guns. Christmas morning Ted and Margie asked me to come down to their store. They gave me a package all wrapped up in red paper. It was my gun set! I couldn't get over it. For months I went around practicing my draw.

Why couldn't Christians be like Ted and Margie, who never went to church? But Christians weren't like that. By the time we moved to Hagerstown, Maryland, I found myself rejecting church and everything it stood for. It was in Hagerstown that I first went to the movies. Though I thought I no longer believed in sin and hell, I shook all the way through the show, half expecting to see Satan himself spring from behind the screen.

When I got home Dad was in the garage building a table for Mum's sewing machine. "Where've you been, Charlie?" he asked me.

It was probably a perfectly innocent question, but I felt my guilt stand out in flames. Bursting into tears I blurted out a confession, and a lot more—my dislike of the pious, Bible-toting hypocrites who attended his church, my longing to be like the other kids at school.

To my amazement, Dad took this outburst calmly. "Charlie," he said, planing down a table leg as he spoke, "do you remember the day, a long time ago back in Scotland, when you asked Jesus to come into your heart? You were very small then, but Jesus hears the prayers of children. I believe He came to you that day, and He has told us, 'I will never leave you.' When Mum and I can no longer help you with the decisions you must make, He will always be there to guide you."

I often wondered what my father thought of his own bold words over the next few years, as my path branched farther and farther from his own. The new direction in my life started, strangely enough, at a church rally, shortly after I turned fifteen. A minister was holding a big evangelistic meeting in Hagerstown and, because I hadn't done much lately to make my folks happy, I went to it. At the close of the service the minister invited the whole congregation to come with him to the local radio station where he was going to broadcast part of his message. I went along with a group of others to the old frame house where the station was located.

I stepped through the door, and my life was changed. The microphones, the earphones, the soundproof studios, the cables all over the floor . . . I didn't understand any of it; I only knew it was the most beautiful place I'd ever seen. When the others left, after the broadcast, I hung behind. I slipped into a side studio and just sat there in the dark, watching the announcer through the big glass wall. It was late at night when I crept through the front door of the creaky old house and walked home through a softly falling snow.

Going to the station became a regular custom for me. I used to sneak over there after school, open the door and tiptoe in. I soon got to know the exact spots on the floor where the boards squeaked and learned to sidestep them. There was a production studio where I could hide, sitting in the dark so that no one could see me. Next to the soundproof plate-glass window was a control panel. I learned which buttons to turn so that the sound came on in my little cubicle. I would sit, wide-eyed, watching the disc jockey in the next room handling records and turntables, keeping up a line of chatter, dreaming that I was that man working so unflappably, talking so smoothly.

One night when I was sitting in the dark a guy who worked at the station walked into the room. He flipped on the light, then stared. I knew who he was instantly—Terry Hourigan. I had listened to him scores of times from my secret vantage point.

"What are you doing here?" he said.

He didn't sound mad. The sight of a kid sitting there in the dark seemed to strike him funny. I didn't know what to say, so I simply told him the truth.

He looked at me for a long time. "Listen," he said at last, "why don't you come into the main studio?"

Fantastic! Terry introduced me to Jack Spielman. And all of a sudden these two men, the fellows who had been my heroes, were my friends. Over the next several months I practically lived at the studio. Terry and Jack and their friends treated me as a sort of mascot. They took me with them on studio assignments. It was with Terry and Jack that I first went to Washington, D.C. It was with them that I first went to a real restaurant and learned how to order food off a menu.

Through them too, I was introduced to music. Jazz, the classics, anything: Copeland, Bach, Mantovani, Percy Faith, Beethoven, Frank Sinatra, Peggy Lee, the Four Freshmen. In 1957 we went to the Newport Jazz Festival to hear Duke Ellington. This was also the first time I saw people smoking pot. A new drug culture,

I discovered there, was beginning to grow up around the music culture.

But in our little studio in the sticks, back in Hagerstown, Maryland, we were content with beer. It was with the men at the station that I started drinking. Not that first year. Everyone knew I'd never had anything alcoholic and no one wanted the responsibility of giving me my first drink. But by Christmastime I guess they just got tired of saying, "No, man, you can't have any." Anyhow, one night when they broke out the Budweiser, I helped myself and no one objected. I didn't think much of the taste, at first, but I enjoyed the grownupness of sitting around the studio with our feet up on the desk listening to Brubeck on one turntable while going out over the air were traditional, mawkish Christmas records.

Thus it was that I became more or less officially attached to the radio station. One day Terry said to me:

"If you're going to hang around here all the time, why don't you help out?"

He started by showing me how to edit the news: the local stories, the national stories, the world news. When he was through he said, "Do you want to give it a try?"

"Are you kidding?"

All of a sudden I was an employee. Terry started paying me a little for getting out records for him and filing them away correctly when he was finished. He gave me what he could afford: three, four, sometimes five dollars a week. But at seventeen, doing the one thing in the world I wanted most, that was a fortune.

Besides, the money was welcome at home. Mum and Dad relented a little toward "the devil's box"—as they still regarded the radio—when they saw that it could put groceries on the table.

Still, this must have been a rough time for my folks. Many nights I would come home wiped out of my mind and stinking like a brewery. I would cross the lawn to avoid our crunchy gravel driveway and tiptoe through the "sanctuary" downstairs. Past all the folding chairs, past the little raised platform where my father preached, past the attendance board with its pathetic tally of Dad's results: "Attendance today: 26. Attendance last Sunday: 27. Offering: $7.06." Up the stairs, drop into bed with my head spinning, pass out.

Finally Dad could take it no longer. He called me into his study and said in his heavy Scots accent:

"Boy . . ." whenever he called me Boy I knew a serious talk was to follow. "Boy, I've raised you in Jesus. Now I've got to let you go. There are things you're doing now which I do not approve of. But you can't hear me and your Mum any longer. Remember what I told you. Jesus is your guide now." He paused to clear a huskiness from his throat. "I want you to know that a day never passes except we pray for you."

But if my folks let me go, the people in the congregation did not. I still came to church in deference to Dad—after all sometimes I made up ten percent of the congregation. And I still got the lectures.

"Charles Edward Ross, how old are you?"

"Seventeen."

"Seems you're a mite small for your age."

They had a way of putting their talons right into the place that hurt most. Yes, I was small for my age.

"One of the brothers saw you coming out of a bar last Saturday night," the nagging would go on. "Don't you know alcohol stunts the growth? And you a preacher's son!"

I knew better than to try to get away. I just stood still and learned my lesson, but not the one they thought they were teaching. For as they lectured, my mind ticked off the number of men in the congregation I knew to be drinkers on the sly.

I had thought their hypocrisy could no longer hurt me. But I was wrong, because now it turned against Dad himself. From whispered conversations after church it gradually dawned on me that they were planning to dump him, to replace him with another, more popular preacher.

An evangelist came to the little house-church to hold revival services for a week. At the end of the week he stayed on. And on. He was preaching Sunday mornings now. "Dad!" I'd say. "Why don't you say something! Why don't you do something?" But that was not the Christian way, Dad answered. Christians were not to hold out for their rights, but to prefer one another in love.

Finally a delegation from the congregation came to Dad and said, "This man is our new pastor." Just like that.

I don't know what Dad's inner reaction was. I could only watch what he did. He stayed right on in the church, sitting now on a folding chair along with everyone else, listening to the evangelist. They let us go on living in the house, so the rest of us had to come to the services too. Then one Sunday a strange thing happened.

The evangelist took his place on the little platform, but no sound came from his mouth.

He literally could not speak. After a while my father stood up and said in a low voice,

"Perhaps this morning I should take the service."

That morning my father preached about love and humility. It was not one of those double edged sermons which really accuses. He actually was preaching about love. And as he preached, the congregation came, in their phrase, "under the anointing of the Holy Spirit." At the close, the evangelist embraced him with tears running down his face. The next day he was gone.

But I didn't forgive so easily. Humility may have been Dad's way; it could never be mine. The whole incident was just one more proof of what I already knew: Christians in general, and those in this town in particular, stank.

New York City—that's where I'd head just as soon as I finished high school. The spring of my senior year, I hitchhiked up there, just to look around. The first thing I did was go to the Empire State Building, pay my fifty cents and ride up to the observation platform. Below me was the city, just above me the huge transmitting tower.

The scene I was forming in my mind was pure daytime radio stuff: the little Scottish runt, picked on and despised, comes to the Big City and takes the broadcasting world by storm . . .

Dad was sick. You could tell that just to look at him. One morning I came into the kitchen and found Anne, nine years old, trying to fix my breakfast herself. In the middle of the night Mum had called a neighbor to drive Dad to the hospital. It hurt that in such an emergency nobody had even waked me up. I'd grown so far from my family I guess no one felt I belonged to it anymore.

Dad was terribly still in the oxygen tent when I reached the hospital. Then I saw that his lips were moving. I knew he was praying and I didn't know how to feel about it. On the one hand prayer stood for a church which I couldn't stand. On the other, I knew that God was as real to Dad in this little curtained-off room as I was. Maybe more.

He opened his eyes and saw me. I leaned down to the speaking vent in the plastic tent.

"Hey," I said, "I like your greenhouse."

He smiled. "I do too," his lips said.

Dad had always talked about how he wanted white hair. Yesterday he'd scarcely had a grey one.

"You've got your white hair, too," I said. I swung the bed-mirror around so he could see, and he smiled again. We were embarrassed together. I could think of nothing to say. This little man who lived for Jesus twenty-four hours a day, this little man who saw good in people where I could see only their faults, how I loved him! How I struggled to find some way to say so. In the end, I couldn't. When the doctor came in I started for the door, but Dad called me back.

"Boy."

His voice was barely more than a whisper and muffled by the plastic canopy.

"Boy, God's got a purpose for your life in this—radio thing."

I swallowed, knowing what it must be costing him to admit that good could come from the devil's box.

"Maybe," the laboring voice went on, "if Satan can use it, God can use it better."

He closed his eyes. The doctor was reaching into the tent, taking Dad's pulse. At last he straightened up and murmured a few words from the doctor's liturgy about how well Dad was doing. Perhaps he'd be going home in a few days. After the doctor left I said to Dad,

"Hey that's great! The doctor says you can go home soon."

Dad opened his eyes. He looked at me. "Yes," he said softly. "I'll soon be home."

He died at two o'clock the next morning. Later Mum and I talked with the nurse who'd been with him. She said that suddenly his face just seemed to fill up with light. He raised his hands and said one word.

"Jesus."

And then he was gone.

When we got back to the house a lot of people were inside, removing things that belonged to the church. Mum, numbed with grief, couldn't grasp what was happening. One man and his wife were even trying to get through the bedroom door with my bed.

Half the stuff they carted off was ours in the first place—like the sewing table Dad had made, and some rose bushes in the side yard. But it was when I saw a bunch of them pawing through Dad's tool box that I went crazy. Those weren't the precious church's tools, they were Dad's tools—the ones he'd built my bookcase with, and the backboard for my basketball hoop, the ones I'd seen in his hands a thousand times. I slammed the tool chest lid down and I did a lot of yelling. I couldn't put my Dad's Jesus and these people together. They told Mum that now they'd be needing a new pastor she'd have to get out of the house. Right away too.

"The sooner the better," I said. "You just keep your crummy hands off my Dad's tools."

There was a low-income government housing project in town. I'd get Mum and Anne in there, and then I'd leave this hick town, with its hick ideas, and I wouldn't ever come back.

That night I went to visit my father for the last time at the funeral home. He was in a wooden box, the cheapest coffin the undertaker had. I looked down at him, in his brown "preaching suit," the startling white hair neatly combed. On the very tip of his nose was a small bright, shiny place. Suddenly it was all back: the wail of the air raid sirens, the darkening city. Then Dad striding into my room, picking me up—how tall he seemed then—the quiet, fearless voice with its deep burr, discussing with God the evening's plans . . .

The last thing I ever did with him was to lean down and rub the end of his nose.

3

I had—quite literally—to keep pinching myself to realize that I was not dreaming. For I was still starry-eyed, and all of this seemed fantastically romantic. I was standing backstage at the Brooklyn Fox Theatre, where New York's most famous disc jockey "Murray the K" was putting on a super-rock show. All the big name rock stars were there. Could it be that I, Scott Ross, from Hagerstown, Maryland, was assistant music director at New York's biggest rock station, working side by side with the great Murray himself? Could it really be that after I had fled to New York on my father's death, trading on a tenuous series of contacts, I'd parlayed this little in five years into a job with all the excitement and glamour I had ever dreamed of?

This was my world, I reflected, as I stood in the wings waiting for my date. I felt totally at home in the behind-the-scenes show biz confusion—people yelling for make-up, people yelling for clothes, people running up and down stairs, music throbbing up from the pit. Even the chorus girls waiting to go on stage in their tinselly dresses looked beautiful to me.

And then the Ronettes came offstage. Behind them thousands of rock fans stomped and whistled. I smiled to myself, thinking that one of these stars was my date tonight. The Ronettes had teased me when I first met them, two years ago: at twenty-two I had still been wearing T-shirts and pullover sweaters, short hair combed straight back from my forehead. They couldn't laugh at me now. Now I was part of the music scene, dressed like everyone else. I looked at myself in the full-length rehearsal mirror: new light blue suit, pink shirt, Western boots, trench coat, shoulder length hair. Not bad, Scott from Hagerstown.

The three Ronettes were waiting for the pandemonium to die down. Nedra gave me a big smile, then they ran back on stage for their encore. They sang "Be My Baby," their big international hit that fall, 1963. For eight weeks it had been number one in the polls. There they were now in the spotlight: Ronnie, the leader, still only nineteen; her sister Estelle, twenty; and little Nedra, their first cousin, eighteen years old and to my mind the prettiest of the bunch. Nedra with her mixture of black, Spanish and Indian blood was petite, amber skinned, high cheek-boned. She was something else too. Naive? Unassuming—I didn't know the word for it. I only knew that in a high-pressure world she was something very special.

Now the girls ran off again and I knew they weren't going back on stage, no matter how long the kids out front roared. As they ran past, Nedra blew me a kiss, and I followed her into the dressing room. Again, I had that too-good-to-be-true feeling as I waited for the girls to get out of their costumes behind the screen. How lucky could you get to walk into WINS precisely at the moment when they had fired an assistant director. They'd needed someone who knew how to program a show. "Sure," I had said boldly. "I can do that."

"Okay, we'll use you on a trial basis."

By the end of the week they hired me and nothing was the same after that. Overnight, because I chose the records the deejays would play, I became an important man to the recording business. Nothing was too good. Promoters took me to Broadway shows, they took me to the Copacabana. They flooded me with records and booze. I loved it. I loved the music. I loved the life—including this grungy dressing room with its peeling walls and the stained sink at the end of the room, and the hot sweaty people running in and out.

"Scott Ross, you look great." I turned around. Nedra had changed to a trim beige suit. Her eyes were so black I couldn't find the pupils.

"You look greater," I said. "Let's get out of here, I want to talk to you about the Beatles."

Beatlemania was just then heating up in the States. I had a dream, and my friend Nedra played a big role in it. I wanted to start a rock radio show of my own. I'd been sounding people out and sure enough there was a station interested. The show would be part music, part interviews with the people who made the music. Through my work I had gotten friendly with The Rolling Stones, Peter, Paul and Mary, Bob Dylan, Jimmi Hendrix, Donovan, The Animals, many others. But I had not yet met the Beatles. And this is what I wanted to talk with Nedra about. When the Beatles, recently, had arrived in the U.S., the first thing they'd asked was: "Where are the Ronettes?"

"If I could tape an interview with them," I said over dinner, "it would really help me sell my show. Do you think you could set it up?"

"Sure Scott. It would be fun. Let's dance."

So we danced. And after a while I shared with Nedra the sense of unreality I felt about it all. "This place even—the candles and the tablecloths. Talking to one of the top girl singers in the country about my own radio show—and you not laughing at me. If you want to know, Nedra, I'm still the kid who snuck into that studio in Hagerstown and sat there in the dark. I can't believe I really know you, and all those other names."

Nedra squeezed my arm. "I know, Scott. I can never get over Ronnie and Estelle and me making $1,500 for half an hour's work. But as for names—people are people, aren't they?"

It worked out just as I had dreamed it would. Nedra and I went to visit the Beatles in Brian Epstein's suite at the Worcester. They were just as easygoing in person as they were in public. Fun to be with, relaxed, ready for a party.

"Listen to Glasgow in his voice," John said. With the Beatles I had instantly lapsed back into the accent I had tried so hard to wipe out. I told them how I'd been teased in grade school for the way I talked. "Do you know what I did when I started working for a radio station?" I confessed to John. "I used to sit in front of a tape recorder by the hour trying to erase the last burr."

"Well never mind," George said, "we might learn to like you anyway."

Somebody had sent up a basket of fruit and their manager, Epstein, sat on the couch sullenly taking a bite from an apple, putting it down and picking up another. Nedra and Ringo were out on the balcony identifying various buildings on the skyline. I knew Nedra and Ringo dated sometimes and it made me feel—I don't know. Irritated. The doorbell rang and a delivery boy brought in four suits of clothes cut to order for the band and sent up by some promotionally-minded department store. The boys held them up to each other, laughed, and tossed them aside.

When at last I asked if they would let me interview them for radio, Epstein objected. I was small stuff and he didn't want to bother. But the boys thought it would be fun. So then and there we taped a good horsing-around interview. And when I walked out of the apartment that day I had one of the top radio exclusives of the year.

Over the next couple of years having my own show exposed me to a side of the music scene I'd only observed from a distance up till now. The hunger of kids for something they weren't getting elsewhere. Love? Attention? Importance, by getting near to what they figured was important? Whatever it was, it was a genuine compulsion that attached itself not only to the performers but to anyone connected with them. Since I talked to the rock stars on my show, getting close to me was getting close to them. Every time I came back to my apartment on Eighty-fifth street knots of teeny-boppers—thirteen-, fourteen-, fifteen-year-old girls—were standing around outside. At first they just stared at me. But as time passed they grew bolder. My mail box was broken into, letters were stolen. One day a girl called me at the radio station and started reading a letter from my mother which I'd never received. It was a warm and affectionate note and the chick insisted that it was from a girlfriend. She didn't believe there was anyone called "Mum," and she was angry because she wanted to be my girlfriend.

Another time I was mobbed in the street outside the studio by a group of these teenagers. They ripped my suede jacket straight off my back. Then several of them grabbed hold of my hair and wouldn't let go. When I finally pulled loose there was blood all down my face. And one evening I was trying to leave a Beatles concert at Shea Stadium, where I had been one of the emcees, when a hundred or more screaming kids surrounded my car. All I could do was run the windows up tight, lock all the doors and wait for the police to rescue me.

So I was really glad when I met Martin. Martin was so rich he didn't know how many millions he had. He was my age, twenty-five, and interested in finding a rock group to sponsor. One day I was talking with Martin about the trouble I had getting in and out of my apartment.

"Why don't you come live with me?" Martin asked. "You can keep your other apartment and stay here as much as you want. We've got three doormen downstairs to keep the kids away."

What a set up. Martin's penthouse was on Central Park South. It was like a Hollywood movie set. Gold furniture. Sofas twenty feet long. Rugs so deep it was like walking through the grass. Picassos on the wall, real Picassos. A view over the park.

And the wildest living I had ever imagined.

First of all it was the girls. Warm young bodies who drifted in and out of our lives for an evening or a weekend, then disappeared into whatever fantasy had brought them.

And the booze. I was already drinking fairly heavily but now it was a morning-till-night round of scotch, gin, vodka, beer, wine, rum, all taken one after the other until I was stoned out of my head.

The first time I dropped pills was with Brian Jones of the Rolling Stones. I think I knew even then that one day Brian was going to kill himself with an overdose. He went at it in a crazy way, mixing ups and downs, red pills, yellow pills, pills with stripes on them.

"You ought to try this," Brian said, handing me a fistful of multi-colored capsules. I don't think he even knew what they were. Somebody had given them to him and Brian was the kind to try anything. It was an early November afternoon in 1965 and we were on the terrace of Martin's apartment. Behind us a party was going on, had been going on for four days. Brian popped four of the pills into his mouth. "Groovy," he said.

I took two and they were groovy, all right. When we walked back into the party a little later I felt like I was the tallest one in the room. Brian wanted to get some pot but Martin had passed out.

"Let's go over to my hotel," Brian said. "I've got some of the good stuff, straight from Mexico."

I had never smoked marijuana, but the mood I was in, anything sounded good. As Brian's chauffeur-driven Cadillac was heading crosstown the street lights began to look brown to me. I figured it was the pills. But then they went out altogether. The lights in the stores were out too.

"What's going on, driver?"

"I don't know, sir."

I rolled down the window. Women were screaming.

"Maybe the world is coming to an end," Brian said.

The traffic lights weren't working and the limousine slowed to a crawl. Automobile headlights were the only illumination on the streets. At last our driver weaved his way through the snarl to the hotel where Brian was staying.

I wouldn't have believed it. In spite of the weird blacked-out city, there was a group of teeny-boppers in front of the main entrance waiting for Brian's Cadillac to come back. "There he is!" they shouted.

"Quick!" said Brian.

He pushed me through the service door and waved to the man on duty. Obviously the guy had been through this before because he had the door locked behind us almost before we were through it. He handed us a candle and showed us how to get up to the lobby by the staircase since the elevators weren't working. The lobby too was candlelit. We climbed a lot of flights to Brian's suite. We were taking our coats off when there was a knock on the door. Brian took the candle and opened it. It was Bobby Dylan with a bunch of people.

"It's an invasion from Mars," said Bobby.

They all came in and we stood at Brian's windows looking out over the dark city. It was wild. It was like Glasgow in the war.

"Let's turn on. What better time. The little green men have landed."

Brian rolled me my first marijuana cigarette. Neither he nor Bobby could believe that I had never smoked pot. I wondered myself why I hadn't. There was certainly plenty of it where I was staying. Martin bought grass by the shopping bag. He had a special machine in his apartment for making filter tip joints. I inhaled deeply. Beyond the window everything was black; only the flicker of the candle danced in the dark glass. By now they were saying on the transistor radio that the blackout was probably nothing more than a massive power failure. But we knew better. It was the end of the world, and we were going out on cloud nine.

Some instinct told me to stay away from LSD. Although most of my friends were dropping acid, and Martin kept vials of it in the refrigerator egg tray, I didn't try it until one day—it was New Year's Day 1966—I met a friend from *Life* magazine outside my own apartment on Eighty-fifth Street. I had not been going back there too often because the teenagers were really incredible. One night I returned to my apartment to find a young girl in my bed waiting for me. She got very angry when I told her to go home.

Anyhow my friend from *Life*, David, and I bumped into each

other on the street just outside my place. He lived nearby and he asked me over because he had some really good acid he wanted me to try.

"This will really open your head up," he said as he unlocked the door. "You'll know new things, Scott. You'll know true things."

"If you eat of this fruit, you will be like God," I quoted, "knowing good and evil."

David stared at me.

"It's from the Bible," I said.

"Yeah? No, man, I mean it. You gotta try this." He went into the kitchen and came back with a piece of sugar soaked with LSD.

If I could have looked ahead I would have let it fall right on the floor.

All the time I'd lived in Martin's apartment, the police had never once bothered us. But one day that same year, 1966, a girl named Susanna freaked out: she went screaming out of Martin's apartment half naked, jumped into the elevator, ran through the lobby and across the street to the park.

At first the rest of us were so stoned we thought it was funny. Then we waked up to what would follow. We ran through the apartment picking up all the grass, pills and LSD we could find and flushing them down the toilets.

Sure enough a few minutes later the police were at the door. That time we were lucky. We were clean.

To celebrate we really did get stoned. Martin was so wrecked he just lay on the floor babbling. Money fell out of his pocket. I reached over to pick up the roll and counted two thousand dollars.

"You shouldn't carry that kind of cash around," I said to Martin, stuffing the bills back into his coat.

"There's more where that came from. Let's take a trip," Martin said.

"We're on a trip, old buddy."

"No. I mean a real trip, on a a-ree-o-plane."

So Martin and I and seven other people got into taxicabs and drove out to JFK.

"We want to go somewhere. Anywhere," Martin said to the not-at-all perturbed face at the counter, handing her a wad of bills. "Someplace interesting, and a plane that's leaving right now."

The girl put us aboard a jet bound for Puerto Rico. We went down to San Juan, gambled till he'd lost the rest of the money, and came back.

We stayed wrecked for several days. Little threads of memory are all I have left:

"Where's the motorcycle, Scott?"

"I don't know."

"Well, you rode it last."

"Yeah? Maybe we better try to find it." But we never did.

Another day we went to see the movie *Goldfinger*. In the movie James Bond drove an Astin Martin. It was a fantastic car "—and named after me," Martin pointed out. He called up the Astin Martin people and asked how much a car like James Bond's would cost. "Fifteen thousand five hundred dollars," they told him.

Martin went to the bank and got a certified check for $15,500 and drove his new car out of the showroom. It was a tricky machine to keep tuned though, and Martin soon tired of it. As far as I know it's still in the garage where he left it one night when it didn't start up right away.

Then we got busted.

I had been writing a newspaper column called *Scott on the Rocks*. On the morning of the bust I'd been on an all-night party with some music friends. I came back to Martin's place at six o'clock in the morning, wrote my column, and fell into bed.

The next thing I knew, the place was crawling with cops.

Either there hadn't been time or no one had been awake enough to get the stuff down the toilet. The police found marijuana and hashish and LSD. But instead of arresting us, they hung around. They stayed all day long drinking Martin's booze and eating his steaks and oggling the girls who were in the apartment. Then around five o'clock in the evening they tried to take him for $20,000.

Martin asked me, "What should I do?"

I said, "Man, you know, if you try to pay them they can get you for bribing an officer."

So Martin said, "OK. Maybe we'd better not do it."

At six o'clock they finally took us down to the Tombs. They fingerprinted us, then stood us in front of cameras: full face, side view, the whole thing. Then they booked us for possession.

We got out on bail a few hours later, and as it turned out—for reasons which were never clear to me—eventually the whole case was dropped.

But the damage had been done as far as my radio show was concerned. I was through. All the years of work, of building my contacts, watching my ratings rise—destroyed overnight. Apparently it was one thing for a performer to be arrested on a drug charge, another altogether for a disc jockey; the deejay was hired by the station, and the station had to answer angry parents.

I was out. At twenty-six there wasn't a rock station in the country which would hire me.

I set to work with Martin trying to build a new rock group which Martin would finance and I would manage. But for the first time I began to ask myself where all this was leading. I remember sitting in Martin's penthouse one night talking with Nedra. I hadn't seen her for a while; she didn't think much of my lifestyle.

Nedra was telling me about the new tour they'd just signed to do with the Beatles next summer. New York, Memphis, Chicago, Montreal, Seattle, San Francisco. I figured she'd be seeing a lot of Ringo.

Around us in Martin's apartment a wild party was exploding, as if there had never been an arrest. Music, scotch, grass, heavy sex. Laughter. Serious, nonsensical monologues. Laughter.

"This is where it's really at," I said.

Nedra said nothing. I looked around at the girls sprawled all over the furniture; I looked at the hangers on, all of them out of their heads, and a part of me asked, "Man, *is* this where it's at?"

David was on the scene again. He showed me some articles *Life* had been running about LSD and the high claims that were being made for the chemical.

"LSD can answer your questions, man."

I started dropping acid regularly. Only I found that when I went into a trip with one question, I came back with five more. Then I had to take more acid to try to get my head straight.

On and on it went. Day after day, dropping acid. Things changed in front of my eyes. I remember being amazed one night because I'd never before noticed that New York was made of foam rubber. Everything—the streets, the buildings, even the trees. I was standing out on the terrace wondering why I'd never realized this before. You could bounce from tree to tree all over Central Park. I swung both legs over the railing and looked down twenty-nine stories to the soft, springy sidewalk straight below. If you landed on your feet you'd bound right over Fifty-ninth Street. Have to aim carefully though: those cars down there were made of metal—everybody knew that. I didn't want to hurt myself.

Just then Martin came out on the terrace. He got both arms around me and hauled me down. "What you want to kill yourself for?" he said, really mad.

But I wasn't trying to kill myself. I was feeling great. After that, whenever I'd read about some acid head jumping out a window, I'd remember . . .

I got into strange fear-filled relationships with people. One night a boy named Jeffrey came over to me and said,

"Do you know who I am?"

As I watched, Jeffrey turned into one of the most beautiful people I've ever seen, all shining round with light. But he couldn't keep it up.

"Yeah, I know who you are. You're just Jeffrey." I felt I had to insist on this.

"Look again."

I didn't want to, but Jeff forced me with his eyes. And as I looked he turned back into the beautiful figure. This time he held the image longer. Now he asked me,

"And who are you?"

"Who am I? I'm Charles Edward Ross."

"Are you? *Do you remember the desert?*"

And suddenly without wanting to, I was lying on the floor, my arms out sideways as if I were on a cross. I lay on the floor, crucified, and I could see through the walls. I could see the people in the next room. One minute they were beautiful and the next they were covered with blood.

"Jeffrey, help me."

"Don't call me Jeffrey. You know who I am and I know who you are."

I was running out of the room. I was Jesus Christ, crucified and running down the street. Only—I looked at my hands—where were the nail marks? Maybe I wasn't Jesus. And then I saw it, across the street. Huge neon letters over a doorway: HOLY ROSS CHURCH. It never occurred to me that there was a C knocked out. To me it was the confirmation that I was the son of God.

I ran all the way to my own apartment on Eighty-fifth Street. The place was full of people. Brian Jones and Bill Wyman of the Stones were there. I locked myself in my bedroom. Brian was banging on the door. "Scott! You okay, man?"

"I'm okay."

"Come on out. We want to talk to you."

"I'm okay."

I opened the door to show him that I was in my head. Brian had on dark glasses and for some reason that scared me. I ran back and lay on the bed. Brian and Bill and some other people came in and tried to talk to me. A stranger sat down beside me. I'd never seen this guy before. He leaned over and whispered into my ear.

"You can't get away from me. *Remember the desert.*"

Now I was lying on the floor again, but I didn't know if it was the same night. Maybe it was another planet. I lay on the floor watching the earth explode. I was on a flying saucer, and that made me doubt a little. Why would I need a flying saucer if I was Jesus?

I thought I better phone Mum to let her know what was happening. How I was Jesus, and all. A girl was in the room and I got her to dial the number in Hagerstown. She handed me the phone.

"Mum?"

"Charles! Are you all right, dear? It's awfully late."

I looked at my hands. There were no nail holes, but that didn't prove anything. "Mum, I can't talk long now. There's so much to do. I've got to fight this Satan thing tomorrow. I've got to go out to Golgotha. But don't worry, Mum, I'll dress warm."

I hung up. In a while the phone rang.

"It's Hagerstown," the girl said.

A man's voice: "This is Vernon Miles."

Miles. I thought a minute. Sure, I knew. The preacher from the church Mum and Anne went to now. He was calling up to bawl me out. I knew the whole sermon before he gave it. He was going to tell me what a good woman my mother was, and how I was hurting her, and then he was going to quote seventy-nine scriptures. Imagine—he was going to quote the Bible to Jesus!

But Pastor Miles didn't preach and he didn't quote anything. "I just want you to know we love you, Scott," he said.

He went on talking: news of the church, how Anne was teaching in the Sunday School this spring. He wasn't blaming me, he wasn't accusing me; he was just loving me over the phone, holding me with his warm, gentle voice. It really blew my mind.

The more he talked the better I remembered him. Glasses an inch thick and a shirt collar several sizes too big. Why did I keep getting this crazy idea, then, that it was Jesus talking to me over the phone? It was Vernon Miles—a hick preacher from a hick town. But try as I would, I kept hearing Jesus in his voice.

It began to bother me.

If Vernon Miles was Jesus . . . then who was I?

4

I came down off that trip very slowly.

For three weeks I was afraid to touch anything—even beer.

Then word came that Brian Epstein was giving us an audition. For months Martin and I had been trying to get Epstein to listen to the group we'd formed. We called ourselves The Lost Souls and our talent consisted of four guys who were so good that it was getting hard to keep them waiting on promises alone.

Now Epstein had agreed to hear us. We met in a dingy studio and had our audition. I could tell just by watching Epstein's face that we were in. At first bored, his expression grew more and more animated as The Souls made their way through the intricate patterns of their hard rock creations.

At the end Epstein said just two words. "You're on."

To celebrate we all got stoned. The celebration lasted a week. By the end of that time we were making plans for The Lost Souls to go immediately to England to begin recording sessions.

The only trouble was that as Brian Epstein and I got further and further out of our heads, each of us went into his own ego trip. We quarrelled and disagreed over every detail of the planning and arrangements.

On the day we went to the airport we were all so bombed we

couldn't find our plane. Special people from the airline were assigned to get us aboard. Finally we were all tucked away.

Except me.

In the passenger waiting room, Epstein and I had our final and most serious fight. I accused him of having an emperor complex; he refused to accompany the group if I came along. "When you get your head straightened out," Epstein said to me, "come join us in England."

I set out to do the exact opposite. I took Brian's limousine back to my apartment. A couple of guys from the Rolling Stones were staying there at that point but I didn't even speak to them on my way to the refrigerator where I kept the acid. I was about to go on a trip like no one had ever gone on before. An average dose is about 250 micrograms. I took 1500.

That trip lasted I don't know how many days with no food and no sleep. I kept hoping I'd reach a white light and, like they said, find God. I saw the white light, but God kept getting away. One day friends came into the apartment and found me stretched out on the floor again.

"Scott, you've really flipped."

They started to pull me up.

"Let go of me. Can't you see that I'm Jesus?"

They let go in a hurry. I crawled up to my knees and started saying the Lord's Prayer, over and over. I was really frightened because the high wouldn't go away. "White Light, who are you? Are you the guru? Are you transcendental meditation? Are you what I learned as a kid?" I did not remember what I had learned as a kid. The confusion was banging around in my head. I didn't know who God was. I was Jesus, but who was God?

Isolated memories.

I was on a motorcycle, roaring at a very high speed up Riverside Drive. There was wind in my face and the buildings raced by in a blur. But for some reason I couldn't keep my balance. I looked at the speedometer needle. It read ten miles-per-hour.

Another time I was on my bike on Park Avenue. The traffic

lights were changing. Green, amber, red. It was beautiful. It was the most beautiful thing I'd ever seen: Green, amber . . . while horns honked behind me, I sat there in the middle of the street, watching the lights change.

What finally yanked me down from the high was a phone call from a girl I knew.

"Scott?"

"Yeah."

"I'm pregnant." Just like that.

I waited a long time. "Yeah," I said. "So what's that got to do with me?"

"You're the father."

"Yeah, sure. I'm the father. Sure."

"Scott, I want an abortion."

I couldn't remember going to bed with this chick. But then I couldn't remember not doing it either.

"How do you know I'm the father?"

"I know all right."

"Sure."

"I want an abortion, Scott."

"No abortion." I didn't know why that seemed so important. "We'll get married. No abortion though."

"I'll call you later," she said, and hung up.

I was off the high, but the fear wouldn't go away. I remember one day I was in a pizza parlor on Second Avenue near my apartment when the whole place started to blow up. The guy opened the oven to put my slices in and I could see inside, how it was swelling up to explode. I shouted a warning to everyone and ran several blocks up the street. The only strange part was, when I walked down Second Avenue the next day, that pizza parlor was still there.

They started following me from the rooftops with telescopic rifles. I'd walk close to the buildings so they couldn't get a good shot. Only that was dangerous too because all the bricks were loose and they were going to drop down and hit me. By the time I'd crouched and dodged my way home I'd be exhausted from being afraid. And that was odd because as a kid, back in Glasgow, I never used to be afraid of anything.

And then on top of everything came a letter from the government: my draft board ordered me to report to Hagerstown for a physical. That really did it. First my radio show, finished. Then my big chance with Epstein and The Souls—blown. The chick with the baby coming. My mind going through changes. And now the lousy draft board.

I couldn't cope with it. The Ronettes and the Beatles had finished their big U.S.–Canada tour and Nedra was back in the city. I called her up. Nedra was the only person I knew who was straight, yet you didn't mind telling her things. I told her about Epstein and how people were chasing me and about the draft board. I didn't, however, tell her about the pregnant girl.

"So I've got to go to Maryland."

"Scott, if you go to Maryland I'm coming along. You need someone with you."

So I had to tell her about the girl and the baby too.

"If you go to Maryland," she repeated, "I'm going with you."

My car had been re-possessed so we were going to go in Nedra's. But when she showed up at my apartment I saw she didn't even have a suitcase. Her mother had been adamant that she wasn't going anywhere with this busted, no-good ex-disc-jockey bum. Nedra had reminded her mother that she was twenty years old now, and simply walked out of the house without her bag or her car keys or anything.

"Scott . . ." she looked at me closely. "You're really messed up, aren't you?"

I tried to meet those deep black eyes but I couldn't.

"Scott, I love you. I've tried not to but I do. I don't know what's going to happen to you. I just know I've got to be around when it does."

She loved me. This kid with everything in the world going for her, and the guy who'd messed up everything he got his hands on. Nedra loved me.

We took a Greyhound bus to Hagerstown. I'd been back to see

Mum and Anne lots of times before, but this time for some reason I found myself thinking about a promise Mum had made the day I graduated from high school. She'd said then that she'd be praying for me every morning and every night. Had she really been praying all this time? Eight years?

Mother kissed me and shook hands with Nedra whom she'd met once in New York. She sat us down in her cubbyhole of a living room, made tea and then asked me how things were. Maybe it was Nedra sitting there—so honest herself, knowing all about me and loving me anyway—but I thought suddenly, why fake it? I told Mum the whole story, this time not leaving out the failures. I sat there rolling joints right in front of her, while she just looked at me, this puzzled expression on her face.

"So that's where it's all been at, Mum; the pregnant girl, the drugs, the broken dreams, the whole bit."

"Charles, I want you and Nedra to come to church with Anne and me this evening," she said.

I laughed. I wasn't going to any church. Especially not here in Hagerstown, Maryland, to Mum's funny little Pentecostal place.

"No, I don't want to, Mum. If you turn on to grass, you won't need to go to church either."

I caught a warning look from Nedra. "You don't have to get fresh," she said.

On second thought, it might be kind of a gas. You know, the little southern, lily-white church with its prissy ideas. Nedra just dark-complected enough to give them fits, and me with my shoulder length hair and my suede suit with the long fringes. And stoned out of my head. It could be a gas.

So that night we all four went to church. Nedra and I sat in the back under the balcony where God couldn't see us. I was laughing my head off at these small town hicks with their crew-cuts and white socks. They were fresh out of the hills all right. I knew their phony-emotional service by heart too.

"Yeah," I said to myself, "here comes the part where they try to make you feel guilty. And now come the soupy hymns to turn you on. After a while someone's going to 'receive a scripture' for the evening." It was going to be very hard for anyone to quote the Bible at *me:* I could return five scripture verses for every one they could dish out. I knew the Bible. I was raised on it. And I wasn't buying.

Up front I could see Vernon Miles, the guy who'd phoned me in New York that time I thought I was Jesus. His trousers were about five inches too short and his socks didn't match. He picked up a Bible.

"Amen," he said. "Let's see what the Lord's got for us tonight." The guy must be blind. He brought the page up to about an inch of his nose, but even with those thick glasses, he couldn't make it out. He handed the book to someone else to read. The passage was from Jeremiah. ". . . I will cleanse them from all the guilt of their sin against me, and I will forgive all the guilt of their sin and rebellion against me. And this city shall be to me a name of joy, a praise and a glory before all the nations of the earth—"

Suddenly Pastor Miles raised both arms straight in the air.

"That's it!" he said. "Whoo-op! Praise You, God!" He jumped. Literally jumped up in the air. "Praise the Lord. Praise You Jesus!"

It was comical. I would have laughed out loud, except that this guy was wiping me out. He started talking about how God doesn't see us in terms of our sins and failures. He said God did not see us that night as we were, sitting there in the pews, but that He saw each of us complete and whole. A praise and a glory—that was the way we looked to God. For some reason I was starting to shake like mad. I wanted to get out of there and turn on some more. But Nedra was gripping my hand. All at once she said,

"Scott, this is for us."

I turned to look at her. To my amazement she was crying, big tears rolling down her cheeks.

At that moment some woman got out of her seat, came over and grabbed me by the arm. "Son, you need Jesus," she said.

I stared at her. She looked exactly like a woman who used to be in my dad's church. I hated her guts.

"Get away from us," I said.

Down front, someone was speaking in tongues. Shouting in

tongues was more like it; I recognized the high-pitched hysterical babble from a thousand church services in my childhood.

From the other side of the room, came the "interpretation" in a kind of wailing chant: "I have directed your steps to this hour. Cast your burdens upon Me, my children, yea, cast them all upon Me!"

What was there in this familiar rigmarole that was making my throat swell, my eyes sting?

"There are two people here tonight," the sing-song wail continued, "who are responding even now to My call. Come forward, come forward, My children! Give your hearts to Me this night!"

"Scott," Nedra said again, "that's us! Those two people—that's us. Scott, let's go forward!"

She tugged me by the hand and I followed. Together we stumbled down to the long kneeling bench that stretched across the front of the church. Mum sat ever so still in a pew nearby, but Anne came up and knelt down beside us. In fact it seemed like half the congregation got up and came to stand behind us. I tried to focus my attention on the grain of the wood in the floor to keep from crying. It didn't work. Tears were falling on my jacket, making blotches on the new suede.

Then Pastor Miles was standing in front of me. He laid his hands on my shoulders. "Your father would be very happy tonight, son."

At the mention of Dad, I really broke down. My mind went back to that hospital room. "God has a plan for your life, Boy." It was almost the last thing Dad said before he died. It freaked me out, thinking about that.

I couldn't take any more. I had to get out of there. Embarrassing as it was, I grabbed Nedra by the arm and forced our way through the crowd standing behind us.

"Let them leave," Vernon Miles said in his warm, loving voice. "The Lord's ways are not ours."

Once again, Vernon Miles caring about me. He was not doing the expected thing, he was caring. By the time we got back to Mum's I was shaking worse than ever. The first thing I did was to roll a joint. Nedra watched me silently, not condemning, just waiting. I offered it to her, but as usual she shook her head. I lay down on the couch, lit up and inhaled.

And immediately sat up, gagging. The smoke felt like it was poisoning me. I coughed. A black ugly substance came up out of my throat. I looked at Nedra, confused and frightened. I coughed again and more of the vile black mess came out of my throat. I jumped up from the couch, ran to the toilet and threw up.

When I got back the phone was ringing. It was the girl with the baby. Somehow she had found out where I was, and she was having a screaming fit because she thought I'd tried to run away. I told her I was coming back as soon as I'd seen the draft board. I also told her what had just happened in Vernon Miles' church. She couldn't understand it, but then neither could I.

"Well, so long," I said to her at last. "Doubtless I'll be hearing from you."

"Doubtless you will, Daddy."

After I hung up I knew I had to get off by myself for a while. "You mind staying here alone?" I asked Nedra. "Mum and Anne'll be back soon."

"Of course not, Scott."

So I left Nedra at the apartment and took a walk through the dark Maryland countryside, rolling joint after joint, lighting up, then throwing it away because of the gagging.

The next day, I went to see my draft board. When they asked if I had ever been arrested and I told them about that bust on drug charges, they wanted nothing more to do with me.

So that was that. We could get out of here. At the bus station Mother hugged me, then turned and hugged Nedra too.

"I want you to have this," she said. She put Dad's Bible in my hand.

I looked at it. I didn't know what to say. Out of the window I saw Mum waving till the bus was out of sight.

A funny thing happened. As we roared along the New Jersey Turnpike, I found myself praying. Actually talking to God. I hadn't done that in years. It wasn't much of a prayer. Sort of a spiritual shrug. "Well, Lord, I don't know what You're doing . . . here I am still stoned . . . not even the Army wants me . . . what good could I possibly be to You?"

As soon as we got back to New York Nedra left to go shopping with Ronnie and Estelle. The three of them were leaving in less than a week for a tour of Germany and Spain. I wandered aimlessly around the apartment. If grass wasn't agreeing with me, there was plenty of booze and acid around. But each time I'd reach for some I'd keep wondering what it would be like to be in my right mind for a change. At last my eye fell on Dad's Bible lying on the bed beside the suitcase, the big black Thompson's Chain-Reference edition he'd loved. I picked it up and thumbed through it. Dad's small, neat handwriting was on almost every page, filling the margins, even squeezed between the lines. I sat down and began to read.

Over the next few days, without understanding what was happening to me, I gulped scripture. I couldn't seem to stop. I would get up early in the morning—which by itself was a miracle—and start to read. It made no difference where I opened the book, it was all like food to a starving man. New Testament, Old Testament—I read about Saul and David and Solomon, the split kingdom, the wars, the exiles, like it was today's newspaper. I raced from page to page, hungry to discover how it all turned out, even though I'd known these stories since childhood.

On the third day, there was a knock at the door. I thought it was Nedra coming to say goodbye, and ran to open it. It was some musician friends full of talk about a big concert they'd just signed for. I tried to get interested, but I had to keep asking them to repeat everything.

As the drinks went round, they noticed I wasn't having any. "Man, what's happened to the party?"

"You wouldn't believe it if I told you."

But I tried to, anyhow. How I couldn't stop reading the Bible. "This book is speaking to me, man. It's talking about what's happening."

"Yeah? That's great. Have a joint."

Saturday I went out to the airport to see the Ronettes off to Frankfurt. Afterwards it was awful. It was like my whole life took off with that plane. Next morning I tried to go to church. I walked into a big place downtown. A phalanx of ushers in white gloves closed in on me. "You'll be very welcome in the Lord's house," one of them said, whispering so as not to break the holy hush, "when you return in appropriate attire." Sure, bud.

Up the street another place let me in. Afterwards I spoke to the minister. I told him I was trying to figure out what this book was all about—I held out Dad's Bible. He told me the church was having their midwinter retreat next month and if I wanted to come I should put down a $200 deposit.

Finally, the third Sunday of looking, I wandered into a funny little place on East Sixty-second Street. The name really grabbed me: Rock Church. Only "Rock" turned out to mean Jesus. It was a great place, though. Nobody asked me for money, nobody griped about my clothes. The preacher talked about the scriptures and he kept answering the very questions I was asking. There were services at Rock Church every day and I started going a lot.

Being a new person in Jesus, that's what I wanted to find out about. Starting fresh. Getting all the old junk behind me. "Therefore if any man be in Christ, he is a new creature"—I found that in Second Corinthians. I liked that. "Old things are passed away," it went on: "behold, all things are become new." Dad had drawn a line under that verse, and already I could tell that part of it was true. I mean—getting up early in the morning to read the Bible, not wanting a joint or a drink, not even thinking about them. That was new all right.

But . . . "old things are passed away"? As far as I could see, most of the old things were still around. The fear whenever I had to walk down the street. I had thought the fear was a chemical reaction, because of all the drugs I was taking. But I hadn't touched drugs of any kind for weeks, and it seemed like the fear was getting worse. Sometimes my heart would pound so hard I couldn't breathe. I even went to a doctor but he couldn't find anything wrong.

Pastor Vick, at Rock Church, said if we felt afraid, all we had to do was pray. Man, it seemed like I prayed all the time. And it helped, some. But this thing sure hadn't "passed away" when I became a Christian.

One night while Nedra was away I was lying in bed around 2:00 A.M. trying to sleep (that was another thing I was having trouble doing), when suddenly a beautiful, glowing, shimmering light entered the room. I started to sit up, all excited because I thought it was Jesus, when this paralyzing fear crept over me.

The light was beautiful, the most beautiful thing I'd ever seen—and yet, if it was Jesus why was my mind suddenly full of terrible thoughts? I pictured an airplane in flames. The plane was burning, falling, with Nedra inside. But I knew it was more than a thought. It was happening, right this minute. I saw the plane crash to the ground and explode, and Nedra was dead.

I wanted to jump up and run to the telephone and find out where in Germany the plane had gone down, but I couldn't move. The light pulsed and glowed. It was alive and it was all-powerful, and if I moved even a finger it would kill me.

I felt sweat soaking the sheet beneath me. I was crying for Nedra but I couldn't lift my hand to wipe my eyes. My eardrums ached my heart was pounding so hard. I watched an hour crawl by on the clock on the dresser. Two hours. And still I lay pinned to the bed and the fear grew and grew.

Dad's Bible was on the dresser next to the clock and I knew it could help me. But it might as well have been on the moon, as far as getting to it. My heart couldn't stand the wild banging much longer. The beautiful light grew brighter, dimmed, grew bright again.

Six A.M. I was stiff from staying in one rigid position so long. My heart still shook my body each time it beat, but it was slowing down. I was suffocating. I couldn't get breath down into my lungs.

Outside the window the palest hint of gray appeared. And suddenly I knew that if I could get that window open, something clean and life-giving would enter the room. It took many more minutes to build my courage, but at last in a single leap I hurled myself

off the bed and tore open the window. I leaned outside for a minute, gulping the icy January air. When I turned around, the shimmering light had gone.

I dashed to the phone. No use calling Nedra's mother: she'd
only hang up on me. So—though it was only 6:30 in the morning
—I dialed Nedra's Aunt Helen, to ask if she had any details of the
plane crash.

And of course there hadn't been any crash.

It had all been my own mixed-up head. Or . . . was it something outside my head, too? Something that wanted to hurt me
and keep me afraid? I remembered Jeffrey and that time when
I thought I was Jesus and he was Satan. What if that had been
more than just drugs, that time, too?

As it turned out, Nedra was back in New York two days later.
The Ronettes had played nine cities in Germany to standing-room-
only houses, then abruptly cancelled the Spanish half of the tour.
"Why, Nedra?" I asked, hoping she'd say it was because she'd
been as desperately lonesome as I had. We were sitting in a Dunkin'
Donuts place which was the best I could afford nowadays. Nedra
seemed tense and tired as she always did after a tour. She stirred
her coffee for the dozenth time without tasting it.

"Scott," she said finally, "there was this guy over there. Part of
the publicity team. He kept telling me this Jesus kick would last
exactly a month. That's what he called it, 'this Jesus kick.' He
kept daring me to go out with him—said he could bring me back
to earth in one evening."

"And—did you go?"

"No. But not because I didn't believe him. The horrible part,
Scott, is that he was right! If I go on with these club dates, the
clothes, the fan magazines, all the rest of it—oh, maybe not in a
month, like he said, but sooner or later what happened in Maryland is going to start to seem crazy."

"Lots of people in music are into Jesus," I said, vaguely. I didn't
know who they were, but I was sure there must be some.

"I know. I kept telling myself that. Maybe it's just me. I mean—

I 'went forward' at a church service. But what do I know about Jesus? This guy would ask questions and I wouldn't have any answers and he'd laugh himself sick. One church service just isn't enough."

Anyhow, she went on, while they were in Germany Ronnie had suddenly announced she wanted to leave the group and marry Phil Spector. Phil was the record producer for the Ronettes. "When she said that, Scott, it was like God opened a door out of a big dark room. Estelle wants to keep on, but she's good enough to get solo dates if she decides to."

And that's how it happened. Estelle started singing alone. Ronnie got married. And Nedra and I began going together to Rock Church.

We went almost every night, partly because we liked it, partly because I wasn't working and every place else cost money. I'd long ago made up my mind never to spend a dime of Nedra's bread. All this while I'd been job hunting, but I was still black-listed at radio stations and I didn't want to do record promotion or anything. Not because I didn't believe in the music, but because my friends in the music world spent all their time stoned and I didn't need it. So I spent the days answering ads in the *Times,* evenings with Nedra at Rock Church. Nedra would arrive from uptown in her white Chrysler Imperial hard-top with its black leather seats, I'd walk from my apartment, and we'd settle down to listen to Pastor Vick.

One bitter cold February evening, I had two pieces of news as I waited for Nedra on the corner of Sixty-second Street. First, I had a job, clerking at Bookmasters. And second, I didn't have a pregnant girlfriend. I pulled Nedra into a doorway out of the wind.

"Guess what? The girl with the baby? 'My' baby? Well suddenly she isn't pregnant anymore."

"What do you mean?"

"I don't know. She just got herself unpregnant and it wasn't an abortion either. Seems it was all a great big mistake. She called up this afternoon to say goodbye."

I looked down at our feet, so close together on the narrow sill.

Nedra was wearing little white boots with white fur around the tops. "Nedra, will you marry me?"

"Of course, Scott."

To Nedra's mother, though, it was anything but of course. To her I was still a strung-out bum in pursuit of her little daughter's fame and fortune. Nedra had turned twenty-one January 27, so she didn't need her folks' consent, but to prove her point she and I agreed that she should put all of her property and income in her mother's name. Nedra would keep only her car. She and I would live on my bookstore clerk's take-home pay of $102 a week. I had often spent that much on an evening.

Nedra and I wanted to get married in Rock Church. Together we went to Pastor Vick and made the plans. The ceremony called for an exchange of wedding rings. I didn't know whether you could buy one ring for fifty dollars, let alone two—but it was all I had, and someone gave me the name of a wholesale jeweler's on the West Side. On my way down Fifth Avenue, I passed Tiffany's. It sure would be great to get Nedra something from there. And all of a sudden it was as if Jesus Himself were telling me to go inside.

"Sure," I said to myself, "just walk right in!" I wasn't accustomed to this kind of nudging and didn't know what to make of it. But I went in anyhow and was wandering around when I heard a voice,

"Hello, there!"

I looked around. There was this guy standing behind a counter.

"Don't you go to Rock Church?"

I didn't recognize him.

"I sing in the choir."

Now I remembered. We talked for a few minutes. Then he asked me if I was looking for something special.

"Frankly, I don't know what I'm doing in here at all. I need a couple of real inexpensive rings. I'm getting married."

"Wouldn't you like something from Tiffany's?"

I laughed. "Yeah. Sure. I'm a clerk in a bookstore and I buy rings at Tiffany's?"

The guy stepped from behind the counter and talked for a while with a fellow in a morning coat. "I think we can do something," he told me. I went out of that store ten minutes later with two gold wedding bands in a little velvet bag. It was unbelievable. I carried that little bag around with me for three days, just thanking God for giving us the best when all I could afford was the cheapest.

We decided to have the wedding just after the regular 7:30 Sunday evening service, so at least there'd be a few people from the congregation there. No one from Nedra's family was coming except one cousin, Elaine, who'd agreed to stand up with her. I knew my mum would never understand my bride's family not being there, so we just told her and Anne we were getting married and didn't mention a ceremony. We did invite some friends from the music and show biz world, but we were pretty sure they wouldn't show up because it was in a church.

But when the night came, to our amazement, there they were, sitting in the back pews, our atheist and freak and Taoist and Eastern mystic friends, all of them under thirty, while no one down front was under fifty. My Jewish friend David from *Life* was there, clapping his hands like an old-time Pentecostal, crying,

"Out of sight, man!"

They were all stoned. The lot of them. The regulars at Rock Church didn't quite know what to make of it—especially Nedra's mini wedding dress—but they were very nice about it. After the marriage service they all wanted to shake hands with Nedra and me, so we stood in the door with Pastor Vick and said "Thank you," and "Yes, very happy," for fifteen minutes. When the first old fellow got through pumping my hand I looked down and there was a crumpled dollar bill in it. "I can't take this!" I said—the guy worked as a janitor on Seventy-second Street.

He patted my shoulder. "You keep it, son. Jesus wants you to have it."

The next person it was the same thing. And the next. Dollar bills, quarters, dimes, one five-dollar bill. "Jesus told me to give you this." Nearly every individual in that procession of garment workers, cleaning women, widows and retired old men left a little money in my hand—some of it, I suspected, carfare and lunch money for the week ahead. If the line hadn't ended when it did, I would have been bawling like a baby.

Afterwards, our musician friends had a surprise for us too: a wedding party at The Scene over on Eighth Avenue. Tiny Tim and a group called Spanky and Our Gang were there to make the music, playing a lot of the songs Nedra and the girls had made famous. It was a fantastic evening—only I had all these quarters and dimes in my pocket, and I kept wondering how much the party was costing.

How come, I wondered, Christians were always the ones with the frayed overcoats, while everyone else had clothes and cars and all the good times they wanted? Christianity had kept my father poor all his life—was it going to do the same for Nedra and me? I looked around at the crowd, dancing, laughing, having fun. How could I tell them, "I'm into something great," when to all outward appearances Christianity had nothing to offer at all . . .

I sat on the sofa in our apartment on Eighty-fifth Street, trying to figure it out. Now that I was a Christian was I supposed to cut my hair, take off my boots, say good-bye to the world I knew best?

That morning I had walked to work feeling great. I wanted to run up to everyone I saw in the street and tell him, "Listen man, let me tell you about Jesus." But—you know. You can't do that.

When I got to Bookmasters, I put on my clerk's face and began selling. After a while, a group of young people came into the store. They kept looking at me and whispering. Finally this boy came over.

"Aren't you Scott Ross?"

"Yeah."

"What are you doing here?"

"Selling books."

"Haven't you got your show anymore? That's too bad. We used to think you knew where it was at."

"Not then, man. But now I'm into something heavy."

"Yeah? What?"

And suddenly I was in a trap. What could I possibly say? It would all come out Christianese, the thing I hated. I had "gone

forward"? I had "found the Lord"? I was "saved"? In the end
I told the kids it was sort of private and after a while they left.

But soon as I had a chance, I went back to the stockroom and
prayed: "Lord, this isn't any good. I want to talk to people like
these. Jesus, You've got to train me. Please."

When I got back a book was lying on the counter. I started to
put it back on the shelf when something prompted me to flip it
open. Next minute I was really staring. There, in a footnote, was
a reference to Hagerstown.

What a crazy coincidence that this writer should mention the
little Maryland town where Nedra and I had first felt Jesus tugging
at us. Was this His answer? He'd gotten through to us once in
Hagerstown. Were we to go back there, back to Pastor Miles'
church, for the rest of the message?

I sat there at the coffee table in the apartment, trying to get it
right. We'd have to move out of this apartment next week in any
case; my year's lease was up, and it was a cinch I couldn't renew
on a clerk's salary. What if I were to quit my job at Bookmasters
and go down and offer my services to Pastor Miles, just whatever
menial jobs he had, while we tried to get to know God better . . .

Which is how, a few days later Nedra and I pulled up in front
of Mum's apartment and began to unpack the Chrysler.

"Hi'ya, Scott."

I turned around there stood Bill Something-or-other, a boy I'd
gone to high school with.

"You paying a visit?" Bill asked.

Man, I said to myself: two minutes in town and already the
hot-shot who made it in New York is having to eat humble pie.

"No, we're staying a while. Bill, I'd like you to meet my wife."

"How d'ya do," Bill said. "Too bad things didn't work out up
north."

"They worked out."

"Sure."

Mum and Anne gave us a warm welcome. Too warm in a way.
Mum couldn't do enough for us, and over the next few days I saw
Nedra wondering where she fitted in. It was always "Char-rles"

with a burr. "Char-rles your bath is ready." "Don't bother with supper, Nedra. I know what Char-rles likes." The Little Scottish Mother Bit, Nedra called it. And then there was Anne. Seventeen now, she was quite literally sitting at my feet to hear tales about the big city. It didn't bode well for our marriage, all the attention I was getting from two women whom I also loved.

Then there was the question of what I should do with my time. I read the Bible a lot and I worked down at the church, sweeping the basement, arranging chairs, helping little old ladies lift things. Which was okay—little old ladies need help. But we never seemed to find much to talk about.

So it all came down to finding a part-time job so we could have our own apartment. One night when Mum and Anne had gone to bed Nedra and I decided to go about house- and job-hunting in a way we'd never tried before.

We'd pray about it.

It was the first time the two of us had ever prayed together and we were so self-conscious we couldn't meet each other's eyes. "Jesus," I said, staring hard at the carpet, "we're having hassles. We can't hack living in this apartment with no privacy. I need work and we need a place of our own. Amen."

It was a pretty weird prayer, but within ten days both parts of it had been answered. I got a part-time job writing commercials and doing news for a nearby radio station. The job paid the grand sum of $22 a week—even Bookmasters had paid almost five times that much—but with the $22 we were able to rent a tiny apartment a few blocks from Mum's. The bathroom was down the hall, the furniture almost non-existent, but it had a new kitchen, and above all it was our own.

Nedra and I were getting ready for bed, the first night in our new home, when I remembered something I'd read in the Bible just that morning.

"Nedra, do you know what we are?"

"Besides a couple of crazy kids?"

"Yeah. Besides that, we're like those lepers who never came back to say thank you to Jesus." So, standing there in the bare little bedroom, feeling, this time, not quite so embarrassed, we thanked God for our apartment and for the job. When we switched out the light it was with a sense of being close to something huge.

Perhaps it was just as well that we did not know what lay ahead.

Maybe the problem was that I expected things to be different now that I was a Christian. And they were different, in a way. Jesus, the Bible, prayer—every day I was finding out about a whole new world. It was me where I didn't see any changes. I remained the same messed-up, self-centered individual I'd been all along. I was still having fear trips—and they could scarcely be drug flashbacks at this late date. I still had the same bigmouth temper that had driven me and Epstein apart.

Only now the person on the receiving end of that temper was Nedra. Moving into the apartment solved things for a few days, then we were scrapping again.

"For one thing, Mr. Scott Ross," Nedra said, "it's like being in a prison around here. I'm not used to being alone. You go down to that church or off to your job and I stare at the walls. I want to go somewhere today. Let's go to a movie. Let's drive to Washington."

And instead of understanding how many adjustments she was trying to make all at once, I'd blow up at her. If I started taking off, how could I keep a job? And if I didn't have a job, that meant moving back with Mum. Nedra didn't need logic, of course, she needed company—but I was too dense to see it.

We had a little respite with a piece of tremendous news. Nedra broke it to me one night as we were walking over to Mum's. It was a lovely evening, the trees pale with new yellow buds. She must have been waiting for just such a setting.

"Scott . . . we're going to have a baby."

Right there on the sidewalk we hugged and danced around like crazy. When we told Mum and Anne they broke out the tin of real Scottish shortcake they'd been saving for Anne's high school graduation party. Things would be all right now. The baby would draw us together and solve all our problems.

But within a week we were shouting again. The strain of getting along on $22 a week, trying to get used to each other, adjusting to the low key life after New York, trying to figure out who Jesus was, getting used to the idea that we would be parents: everything seemed to work together to move our tensions into a new pitch. Becoming Christians hadn't changed anything, it seemed to me— except to make things worse. We'd lost touch with most of our friends, we were quarreling with each other, we were broke—and then as if things weren't bad enough, along came the news of the death of a friend.

I was having tea with Mum in her kitchen. On the table sat her radio, one I had sent her from New York. I flipped it on for the news.

"This late word just in," the announcer was saying. "Beatle manager Brian Epstein died this morning in his London apartment. According to police, the cause of death was an overdose of drugs."

I must have gone white or something, because Mum put down her cup. "Are you all right, Char-rles?"

"I knew him, Mum. We fought, but we were friends just the same."

Mum reached over and patted my hand. "I'll heat up some nice hot broth. It's good and strong and full of comfort."

I didn't want the stupid stuff. How many of our friends were going to die of drugs? I thought of Brian Jones. Jimi Hendrix. Peter Yarrow's brother. Talk was that all of them were in trouble. And what about a thousand young people whose names I didn't know but whose faces I'd seen, staring up at the stage in a darkened theater, milling around a stage door after a concert, standing in the street outside some hotel entrance. People that I, along with the rest, had helped convince that drugs were a great scene. Suddenly and without warning, I burst into tears.

"It's no good, Mum. Here's Eppie gone. He gets in the news, but how many are there no one ever hears about? I know these people, Mum. They're my people. I've got to find some way to help them."

Mum picked up the untouched bowl of broth. "I hope you and

Nedra patch things up soon, Char-rles. If you can't manage your own life, how can you hope to straighten out somebody else's?"

I knew Mum was right. The week before, after a particularly noisy argument, Nedra had packed a suitcase and flown up to visit her cousin Estelle in New York. After work Monday I drove up to see her.

Estelle's apartment on Riverside Drive was all antique mirrors, sectional couches and distant hallways. Nedra and I started out lovey-dovey enough, but within an hour I was yelling again. This time the issue was where the baby would be born. Her obstetrician was urging her to decide. Nedra wanted to be in New York, near her mother. I asked what was the matter with the hospital in Hagerstown. That was where she belonged. I had a job, I could support her: her place was with me.

And then all at once I didn't have a job. The day I got back from visiting Nedra the station manager came into my office. "Ross, we like your work."

"Thank you."

"We need a full-time air man and you're it."

"Well, ah—can I think about it?"

The manager looked at me quizzically. "You mean you might not want the job?"

So I had to tell him about the church and how the whole point of coming to Maryland was to spend part of every day over there.

"Well, take it or leave it, fellow. We don't need a part-timer anymore. Either full time or not at all."

He left, and so did I, to draw my severance pay.

When I called Nedra that night I was in great confusion. She'd *have* to stay in New York now: her breadwinner wasn't even pulling down $22 a week. "Lord Jesus," I prayed as I put down the receiver, "was it just my own idea, coming to Hagerstown? I thought down here You could show me Your plan for my life. Maybe, Jesus, You don't have any plan for me?"

That really scared me—thinking that maybe Jesus Himself couldn't make anything good out of me. Maybe I'd gone too far the other direction. Maybe when you played around with evil—on purpose, over a period of time—the evil got inside you, and you wouldn't ever be free of it. With me it had been drugs and booze and illicit sex. With someone else it might be greed, or hate, or stealing, or witchcraft. Whatever it was, maybe if you really gave into it, then even when you stopped doing it, the evil thing went on controlling you.

What scared me was that this other thing, this evil thing, was following me now even into church. I'd be sitting there, trying to pray, trying to find God, when a black suffocating something—like a plastic bag—would close over me, cutting off the air, stifling me. It was getting so I hated to enter the church. But I didn't know where else to look for Jesus, so I kept going. And it was there, the Sunday after I lost my job, that the thing happened which at first I thought was going to be the answer.

All my life of course I'd known about the Baptism in the Holy Spirit. My dad taught that it was a natural part of Christian experience, and that speaking in tongues was a normal sign that it had occurred.

Maybe—only it sure had never happened to me. I still remembered an awful experience when I was fourteen. My folks had sent me to a summer camp in New Jersey run by Pentecostals. It was okay, except every night you had to attend a service in a wooden building literally with sawdust all over the floor. Well, one night a group of grown-ups surrounded me and pushed me down on my knees and began screaming and yelling at me to "receive the Baptism." My nose was full of sawdust and I was sweating and embarrassed, and at last to get away from them I went "Bugla, bugla, bugla" and some other nonsense sounds. And the guy who had his hands on my head sang out, "He's got it! He's got it!" and everyone began crying and praising God, and I split out of there as fast as I could.

Since that night I'd never once prayed for the Baptism, and I certainly wasn't praying for it now. It was Vernon Miles' regular Sunday evening service, only this one turned out to be unusual. Every now and then someone would move forward to the kneeling rail where he would begin weeping for his sins. Soon the whole congregation was down front, crying out to God.

Well, I thought, okay, that's how I feel too at times—certainly I've got as much to cry about as anyone. So I went forward and knelt down, only I couldn't produce any tears. I tried thinking about everything that was going wrong: Nedra up in New York, and me with no job, and not seeing deep changes in myself, and stuff out of my past still pushing me around. Only, with every thought would come a different one, like: I'm sure happy Nedra married me. And I'm glad we're going to have a baby. And I'm grateful for Pastor Miles and this church—until before I knew it instead of weeping I was praising God for everything I could think of. The cushion beneath me so my knees didn't hurt. The old lady wailing away next to me. This warm summer night. Just being alive.

And all at once to my horror, up from my throat came a deep, loud laugh. I clapped my hands over my mouth. Laughing in church—when I was a child to laugh in the Lord's house was even worse than smoking or listening to the radio. But the laughter kept bubbling up inside me, swelling my chest till I thought I would burst. I tried to force it down, but it kept rising until I wanted to shout for joy. I took my hands away from my mouth to say, "Praise You, Jesus"—but the sounds that came out were like no language I'd ever heard. Joyful fluent phrases rushed up, expressing a love and wonder too deep for words.

How long I praised God in my new language I don't know, but gradually I became aware of other voices praying all around me. The congregation had again gathered to stand behind me. "Thank You, Jesus," one man said, "for giving our brother the Baptism in Your Spirit."

So that's what it was! I thought back to that hot night in New Jersey, the grunting and sweating, the forced effort. The real gift—how freely and graciously it had come . . .

For a while, as I say, I thought this would be the end of my struggles. With God's Spirit coming into my life, things would be different at last.

But they weren't. Differences, sure. A lot of them, and they kept getting bigger. Praising God was a whole other thing, now that I had a prayer language to do it in. I started understanding the Bible like I never could before—and remembering verses when I needed them.

One night after I'd talked to Nedra on the phone I was sitting up in bed praising God. Nedra was staying at her mother's now, and with the baby coming I guess her mother had decided the marriage was here to stay. Anyhow her mom had talked to me on the phone too and been real friendly, and I was thanking God for that and a lot of other things, and pretty soon I began to thank Him in tongues and even to sing in tongues which was a really fantastic experience.

And suddenly right at the foot of the bed was this glorious shining light. This time the light was in the shape of a man and it spoke to me. Incredible as the whole experience was, I sensed somehow that it was "real." I'd had hallucinations when I was on drugs, but this was different. My head was straight, all my senses normal. What the voice said was, "I am your Lord."

Well I was amazed and wondering why God would appear to me, of all people, when this little thread of doubt crept into my mind.

"You are my Lord?" I said.

"I am your Lord and your God and you are to worship me."

But still something about it wasn't right. And then I knew. The joy and love I'd been feeling minutes earlier was deserting me, and in its place was fear. That cold, paralyzing fear I'd known in the apartment in New York, hidden this time, but lurking somewhere within that dazzling light.

And all at once into my mind came a passage of scripture I had read days before in Second Timothy: *For God hath not given us the spirit of fear; but of power, and of love, and of a sound mind.*

I forced myself to look straight into the light:

"Are you my Lord *Jesus Christ?*"

For an answer the glorious figure grew brighter still, showering the room with light like a Fourth of July sparkler. And at that thought I almost laughed aloud. Why, it's like a vaudeville trick, I thought. The lord of the universe doesn't need to resort to cheap theatrics!

And now into my mind crowded scripture after scripture, complete with chapter and verse:

First John 4:18: *There is no fear in love; but perfect love casteth out fear; because fear hath torment.*

James 4:7: *Submit yourselves therefore to God. Resist the devil, and he will flee from you.*

Staring down the thing at the foot of my bed I hurled the verses at it like I was trying to drive off a wild animal with stones. It glowed and swelled a few more times, then grew fainter, and finally vanished altogether.

Man, then I really did praise God! I got up and marched around that bare little apartment like I was at the head of an army. I saw what the Spirit was doing—He was giving me tools to fight with. Tools of discernment. Tools of knowledge. Tools of faith.

Only . . . I would have to *use* the tools He gave. He wasn't going to do it for me. And He wasn't going to change me overnight into some kind of spiritual prodigy. I was still walking around in a body that remembered, and felt, and reacted. To that degree although I was different I was also the same person I'd always been. I could block His activity, miss His message.

Certainly I did not recognize a quite casual invitation at church one day as coming from Him. One of the men asked me if I'd like to drive to Baltimore with him that afternoon to attend a meeting of the Full Gospel Business Men's Fellowship, a group of charismatic laymen.

I said yes, and then spent the trip wondering why. What could a group of middle-aged businessmen have to do with my situation? It was young people I tuned in with. Whenever I drove up to New York to see Nedra, I'd stop to pick up the fellows who stood at the entrance to the turnpike. I'd have the car radio set at a rock station and right away, we were talking music. When finally the guy asked me something like, "So, what are you into?" and I answered, "Jesus," there'd never be an embarrassed silence. Instead, there'd be real interest like, "Wow, man, that's heavy. Jesus. How'd you get into that?"

It all came so naturally—coupling music with talking about Him . . . So what was I doing in this drafty cafeteria in Baltimore? I had plenty of time to wonder about it because the main speaker—a guy named Pat Robertson—was delayed by a storm. When he did get there and began to speak, everyone in the audience seemed to know already what he was talking about. He kept referring, in his deep Virginia drawl, to "our Christian TV station," and "our Christian radio station."

Christian radio station? Christian TV station? I could just picture it. Any station run by this Hollywood-handsome square in his neatly pressed suit, was certainly not going to be my kind of outfit. The guy, I was sure, would be an ultra-conservative southern super-dude. I could just see his chalked face if some long-haired people from the rock culture showed up at his sanctified station.

So why did I go up and talk with Pat Robertson after the meeting? Why did he seem so interested when I told him I had been in radio myself?

"What've you done?"

I told him. And then for some reason I also found myself telling him about the music-centered people I knew, how hungry they were, how lonesome, how suicidal, even, some of them.

"Listen," Pat Robertson said, "would you come down to Portsmouth to do a talk show with me? I'd like to hear more about these friends of yours."

Which is how it happened that a few days later I was driving through Portsmouth looking for the headquarters of the Christian Broadcasting Network. I pulled up in front of a garage-like building which housed the offices of WXRI radio, and a few moments later was sitting with Pat Robertson in the studio. We talked on the air about the generation of young men and women like Nedra and me who were trying to say something about themselves and their world through their culture and their music.

We were still on the air when Pat's secretary stepped into the studio and handed him a letter. Pat read it to himself, then said into the mike: "This is a real coincidence. Here we are talking about drugs and alternate life styles and in the morning mail comes this letter from a college girl who asks why we never speak about these things."

Pat read the letter aloud, all but names and places. The girl had been involved in drugs and sex and wanted to know if religion had anything better to offer.

When the program was over, Pat and I talked again about the timing of that letter. Was it a nudge from God? Maybe we were to start a music-and-talk show designed to reach people just like this girl. But, you know, ideas are easy to come by. We shook hands in the hallway and said the usual things like, "We'll be in touch."

And then, out in the parking lot, a sensation of fear swept over me. I got in the car and leaned my head back. The sides of the car began to melt, turning soft, turning to rubber. I didn't see how it could be a chemical phenomenon: by now I'd been off drugs over five months.

I ran back into the studio. The floor, the walls, were spongy and sagging. The receptionist in the hallway looked at me. "You all right?" she said. She jumped up from the desk. "No, you're not all right!"

The girl ran down the hall calling, "Pat! Pat!"

Pat and two other guys showed up. Without asking questions they, the receptionist and a couple of secretaries formed a circle around me. "Satan, you foul enemy," said Pat in a voice which rang with authority, "we stand together in the power of Jesus against this attack. This man is no longer yours! In the name of Jesus, we command you to leave him alone!"

Even as he spoke I felt the dizziness lift, the numbness in my hands and legs disappear, the fear pass.

I was stunned by the speed of it. I knew these fear attacks, knew how long it took to recover from one of them. With Bible verses, with prayer, even with prayer in tongues, I'd never fought free in under four or five hours. But this release had been almost instantaneous. What was the difference? "We stand together," Pat had said . . . I wanted to ask him about it, but he was talking eagerly on about the new show idea.

"You know, Scott," he said, "Satan only fights what threatens him. I think this attack is a sign that our conversation a minute ago was important. Think some more about a music-and-talk show for CBN, would you? Pray about it. Talk to your wife about it."

It was obvious that Pat regarded that circle of believers in the hallway and the instant answer to prayer as normal procedure. All the way back to Hagerstown I puzzled over those words. We stand together . . .

I did call Nedra in New York that night. I tried to present a flat and neutral picture of the radio show idea, but I wasn't fooling anyone. Nedra laughed.

"You've made up your mind, haven't you, Scott?"

"Yeah, I guess I have."

That weekend I drove up to see her. Martin was back from England and Saturday night we went down to his apartment on Central Park South. It was the same old scene. Acrid smoke so heavy you could get high just breathing, bottles of booze on every table top. Besides Martin and the perpetually present, vague-faced girls, all the members of the Lost Souls were there. We got a terrific welcome.

"Nedra! Scott! We thought you were dead."

"Someone said you were in a monastery."

They were delighted to see that Nedra was pregnant, and proposed that we celebrate by getting stoned. There was great confusion when we refused.

"You mean you've stayed clean?"

"We've got all the high we need, man," I said.

They asked a lot of questions, but I didn't feel like they were listening to the answers. They wanted to talk about the troubles The Souls were facing after Eppie's death.

Nedra's doctor said no late nights, so after a while I took her back to her mother's. I felt restless so I set out walking—nowhere particular, just roaming miles and miles through the city. All at once I noticed a street sign. Sixty-eighth Street. I was just around the corner from Rock Church! My heart raced. I'd go there. I'd go visit Pastor Vick!

I started to run. There, tucked away among the elegant townhouses was the little church that had meant so much to Nedra and me. I smiled, remembering again the wild group of friends who had showed up for our wedding. I raced up to the door and put my hand on the doorknob.

It wouldn't turn.

I tried again. I knocked. I pounded. Then as a lone passerby stared at me strangely, I kicked the door. No one came.

Even Rock Church, the best church I had ever known, was locked tight.

Why should this have been so hard on me? Rationally, of course, no church was going to be open at three in the morning. If you didn't lock up a church in New York, winos turned it into a latrine.

But understanding didn't help. What I was experiencing had nothing to do with reason. I found myself lumping Rock Church together with the jolly group of hypocrites who tried to kick my father out of his church, or the people who told me I could come to their service when I was in "appropriate attire."

They made me sick. All of them. None was any different.

I started back uptown, and all the way I was fighting tears.

While I was in New York I wanted to get some material for the new talk show. Nedra and I thought Times Square would be a good place to do a series of interviews with kids. What did they say their problems were? Were they as turned off by the churches as I was?

We strolled through Times Square with our tape recorder, stopping college students and high school dropouts, long-hair types and guys in uniform. Every one of the people we interviewed was searching for something and said so; not one even considered looking for it in a church. They were hungry, open, eager to talk. With the hum and honk of traffic as a background, they spoke about drugs, sex, the war in Vietnam, the establishment.

We recorded a dozen conversations, then boarded the Eighth Avenue bus to go back to Nedra's mom's. And it was there, on the city bus inching its way uptown, that the strange thing happened.

I was staring past Nedra out the window, thinking about the talks we'd just had, when the side of the bus just seemed to dissolve. At first I was scared, thinking I was having another Satanic attack. But this was nothing like that: I felt no fear, in fact I felt strangely at peace. Only—a movie was unrolling before my eyes.

I blinked but the scene remained. What was happening! The set for the "movie" was a large, barny kind of room that was never closed—somehow that was the first thing I knew about it. And this huge room was packed with people like the ones we had just interviewed, young men and women from the lonesome generation, sitting and standing in a great circle. On a raised platform a group was playing. It was a good, new sound. I could even hear lyrics and to my astonishment, though the sound was contemporary, the words were all about Jesus.

Just as suddenly as it had come, the picture vanished.

I sat quietly for a while wondering what that was all about. For lingering, as a part of the memory, was a feeling that I had seen, not an imaginary scene, but a place which actually existed—even if only in the mind of God.

As we lurched uptown I told Nedra about the vision. She took it very seriously.

"Where was it all happening?"

"I don't know."

"Down in Virginia?"

"I don't know."

"Maryland?"

"For gosh sakes, Nedra, stop bugging me! I told you twice I don't know. It was just a big old room, like a loft."

Nedra sat back, smarting under the lousy temper I still could not control.

But as the bus ground along, I couldn't forget my vision.

"It is 'my' vision, isn't it, Lord?" I asked silently. "You gave me that picture, didn't You, so I'll know it when I see it?"

But the only answer was the gasping of the air brakes.

In many ways, the work at CBN was everything I'd wanted. The talk-and-music show caught on, and I really enjoyed it. I enjoyed the talk part, that is. College students would call in and we would rap over the air. People were meeting Jesus and getting help with their hang-ups right on the program. The letters that came in were unbelievable. "Last Tuesday night I was thinking about suicide. But I heard your program where that blind woman called in, and I decided maybe my problems weren't so earth-shattering after all." Or from a sixteen-year-old: "I'd been on speed for three months, afraid to come down off the high because the low was so awful. The first night I tuned in your show, I came right off and I never did crash!"

It really freaked me out, thinking of the possibilities in a show of this kind. But I almost had to forget the music side of my format. I just couldn't find any Christian sounds that I liked. It was all Hammond organ and bird-whistle music. I couldn't believe how bad most of it was. I'd sit in the studio with the earphones on, playing record after record, trying to find something I wouldn't blush to put on the air. Not only was the music awful but the lyrics spoke some kind of private language only a real in-group could understand.

One morning after staff prayers at the studio, I complained about how bad the music was.

"Have you ever heard of Ralph Carmichael?" Pat said.

"Sort of."

"Try some of his music."

And it was good, certainly the closest to a contemporary sound I could find anywhere. But how much Ralph Carmichael can you play? Then I had an idea. I remembered a conversation I'd had recently with Noel Stookey—the "Paul" of the folk group Peter, Paul & Mary. When I'd told Noel about the new show he seemed to understand what we were driving at. What if I talked about that visit with Noel on the air, then played some of the trio's music.

Wow. The first record was still on the turntable when the call buttons on the phone lit up like a computer panel; it seemed like every parent in Virginia was calling to complain about "protest music" going out over a Christian station.

But phone calls were not the end of it. A little later the studio door burst open and a red-faced, furious guy rushed in and jerked my power-supply cords out of the wall. "You . . . you . . . if you play any more of that sin music may God strike you dead!" We finally got the guy out of the studio but when Pat heard about it he made the decision: "No more 'Peter, Paul & Mary.' "

Pat seemed to accept this kind of thing as part of the job, but I seethed for days. It was just as well it was time for me to go up to New York where Nedra was due to enter Columbia Presbyterian Hospital. Right then I couldn't have cared less if the whole state of Virginia dropped into the Atlantic Ocean.

September 29th, 1967, we discovered whom Nedra had been carrying—it wasn't "Christian," it was "Christina." Nedra Kristina we named her. I couldn't get over how tiny she was, lying in that little cart thing, so alone. I had to go right back to Portsmouth; Nedra and the baby would go to her mother's for a couple of weeks when they left the hospital.

I was on the air the evening of October 4th when the telephone call came from Nedra.

"Scott, something terrible . . . terrible . . ."

Between sobs, I got the story. Nedra's mother is a practical nurse: almost as soon as Nedra and the baby reached her apartment she had spotted something peculiar about Nedra Kristina's eating pattern. When she phoned the hospital a nurse tried to reassure her that babies were often upset after being moved. But when Nedra Kristina began to vomit, Nedra and her mother didn't ask any more questions. They wrapped the baby up and took a taxi to the hospital where the doctor re-examined her. "Scott, there's something wrong . . ." Nedra began to cry again. "She's all twisted inside. They may have to operate, and they say there's not . . ." Her voice broke off.

I went back to the microphone and, my own voice none too steady, told our listeners what I'd just heard. And all over the state, people who a few days earlier I'd consigned to the bottom of the sea, began a round-the-clock prayer campaign for our baby. As I set out for the airport, the staff of CBN again formed a circle around me in the hallway. "As the body of Christ we send you on this mission," said Pat. "Under Him you have authority in your family. Use that authority to stand against the evil attacking your child."

Authority. We send you as the body. Once more I had the feeling I had witnessed something I could not understand, but something that was important. What did Pat mean by— The telephone rang.

"For you, Scott. New York."

It was Dr. Francis Roe, the head of pediatric surgery at Columbia Presbyterian. He wanted permission to operate immediately. "It's the only chance," said Dr. Roe.

Nedra met me in the hospital foyer. The operation was over. Together we went up to the recovery room. Nedra Kristina lay on her back in an incubator, intravenous tubes lacing that tiny body. Her eyes were closed and she was panting. Airtight vents were built into the sides of the incubator. I put on sterile gloves, reached through these and placed my hands on my baby daughter. "Lord

Jesus," I prayed aloud, "I don't understand it, but I take this 'authority' I have from You, and I claim complete wholeness for this little girl."

Next morning after Dr. Roe's rounds, it was "too early to tell." The next day and the next he remained non-committal—though the very burr of his Scottish accent was comforting to me. By the time I returned to Portsmouth at the end of the week he had progressed to ". . . some months in the hospital before we could let her go home."

And all the while our radio family was praying the Storming Prayer. "Storm heaven with us, won't you, folks?" Pat would say. "Nedra Kristina is making progress."

At the beginning of the third week, Nedra phoned that Dr. Roe was bringing other doctors around to visit Nedra Kristina. "I want everyone to see," he'd say, picking up our baby. "This is a miracle I'm holding in my arms."

What a day it was when Nedra and I were able to go on CBN-TV and show everyone the baby they had been praying for. "Why was our child spared when another one dies?" I said into the camera. "I don't understand that. I only know that you and Nedra and Nedra Kristina and I will always belong to one another because of your prayers."

As soon as Nedra got to Portsmouth we'd gone house-hunting. Although a few people gave her deep-olive complexion a double take, no one refused to show us an apartment. We found a three-floor townhouse—complete with cathedral ceiling in the living room—for only $75 a month. The only catch was, it was unfurnished.

"If anyone has a spare orange crate, let us know," I told the people down at CBN.

I didn't know what I'd said that made everyone start laughing. "It's Jesus," Pat explained. "The way He does things. Last week CBN bought an old house with some furniture in it no one knew what to do with. Help yourself."

So we came into a set of chairs and a dining room table and a sofa and some lamps and a mattress. No bedstead, but the mattress went fine on the floor. And it was in our new home, during my prayer time in the morning, that the strange thing began.

I was still reading the Bible before work each day, but now in the quiet time afterward, something new was happening. Words would keep popping into my mind. Urgent, forceful words, with a funny "feel" to them, almost as if they were alive and trying to be born. One day three quarters of the way through the book of Job, I came across a perfect description of what I was experiencing. "Behold, my heart is like wine that has no vent; like new wine skins, it is ready to burst. I must speak that I may find release; I must open my lips and answer."

That was exactly what it felt like. At the office I described the feeling to Pat. He leaned back in his chair.

"It could be what the Bible calls 'prophecy,' " he said. "You know, speaking for God—God's words using a human throat and lips. Why don't you experiment and see? Let the words come out. You'll find out quick enough whether or not they come from God."

With this encouragement, I found out all right. I found out what an idiot one human being can make of himself. It was a few days before Christmas, 1967, and Nedra's folks were coming. Nedra was really into Christmas and birthdays and family times like that, and she wanted the place to look as nice as possible. The trouble was, even with the furniture from CBN, the rooms were still pretty empty. One day I came home from the office, opened the front door, and there towering over me was this young sequoia, a Christmas tree, thirteen feet from the floor to the living room ceiling.

Nedra was standing on a chair stretching up on tiptoe to hook a popcorn chain over one of the branches. "Oh Scott, here! Help me. Isn't it great!" She handed me one end of the chain. "We may not have a bed but we've sure got a Christmas tree! Doesn't it look fantastic!" On and on she went, excited as a child.

As I walked around the tree, looping popcorn, I saw how Nedra had thrown herself into this thing. She had glass balls and tinsel icicles and cranberry ropes and colored lights and all sorts of stuff all over it. I could tell how much it meant to her, which made what happened next all the more appalling.

For the next day at work I had a phone call from a woman complaining about hearing "The Christmas Tree Carol" over CBN. The custom of decorating trees, she informed me, was a heathen practice which the Bible specifically condemned. Well, I thanked her for calling, and forgot it. You know, we got all kinds of weird calls.

But that night, with a sleet storm howling outside, I sat in our living room looking at that giant tree. Again those urgent, compelling words started forming themselves in my head. They even had a faintly Elizabethan ring.

"Verily, I do not look gladly upon this tree in the house of My people, for this tree is an abomination in My sight."

As Pat had suggested I spoke the words out loud, then glanced uneasily toward the kitchen where Nedra was feeding the baby. I could just see her face if she were to hear her beautiful tree called "an abomination." I sighed and turned back to the day's stack of Christmas cards. "Season's Greetings from Your Diaper Service." I looked up at the tree again. It was a creepy kind of night, windy and cold with sleet rattling on the windows. It seemed to me almost as though there were an unwanted presence hovering in the room.

"Yea, the presence you yourselves brought in with that heathen tree!"

The wind moaned around the corner of the house. I sprang up from the sofa, groped among the branches of the tree till my hands closed around the trunk, and without even stopping to unplug the light cord from the wall, started dragging it toward the front door. Balls fell off and broke beneath my feet, tinsel got in my mouth. Nedra, with Nedra Kristina in her arms, reached the room in time to see me haul the tree over the threshold and send it crashing down the front steps, electric cord trailing behind. It skidded across the frozen sidewalk to the gutter and I stepped back inside, brushing off my hands against my trousers.

Only then did Nedra find her voice. "Scott Ross, have you gone stark, staring MAD?"

"Not mad, my dear. Prophetic. God spoke to me very clearly just now about that tree, and I have been obedient."

She stared at me. "He spoke to *you* about *my* tree? My lovely beautiful Christmas tree?" She was too angry to cry. "And you acted, just like that, without even discussing it?"

"You don't understand about prophecy, Nedra. Prophecy means that God has spoken—and when God speaks you don't run around checking it out with people."

"Now Mr. Scott Ross is into prophecy. What's my mother going to say when she sees our Christmas tree out on the sidewalk?"

Even I could see that this scene was bouncing off the wall. I picked up the few balls that had not broken and tried to decorate the mantel. But when Nedra's mother and father, her Aunt Good-Good and her Aunt Oretha arrived later in the week, it was to find a bare living room and a very confused young couple.

Nor was that the end of it. Just a few days after the tree episode I caught a newscast at the station which told of a group of American Indians trapped in a snowstorm out in Arizona. On the talk show that evening I made an appeal for clothing, and it was then that I received a second "prophecy." Right in the middle of the show I got another "word" from the Lord: I was to chuck everything and go out personally to Arizona to minister to the Indians.

When I came home to Nedra with this incredible piece of news she looked at me as if she truly feared for my sanity. Here we were with a brand new baby and a brand new home, and I suddenly announce that we are going to leave Portsmouth, abandon all our radio and music training, and go out to work among people whose problems we know less than nothing about.

But sure enough, while I was on the air the next night talking about the Indians a man telephoned to say that he too had just heard from the Lord. "You, Scott Ross," he intoned, "are supposed to go out to Arizona to work with these neglected children of God."

What else did I need! I'd had a word from the Lord and here

was the confirmation of what I had heard. The only thing that bothered me was the logic of it. I knew a lot about people who were alienated from the traditional churches, and in radio I was finding a way to reach them. But what did I know about Arizona Indians? The farthest west I'd ever gotten was West Virginia. I didn't bring this doubt up with anyone, though; I had taken a stand. The Lord had spoken, we were going to obey.

And then little Nedra Kristina exploded the whole house of cards.

Nedra was valiantly trying to cope with parents, aunts, friends dropping in, no furniture, no Christmas tree, a new baby, and Mr. Scott Ross who was prophesying. One evening there were more guests than chairs so we all went up to our bedroom and sat around on the big mattress on the floor, singing Christmas carols. Nedra Kristina lay on her back in the center of the group, fists and feet waving.

And all of a sudden into my mind popped a portion of scripture I'd read in Matthew that very morning: "Out of the mouth of babes and sucklings thou hast perfected praise."

I looked at Nedra Kristina.

I let my voice drop an octave and pronounced that out of the mouth of this babe we were about to hear the praise of God. In English.

Nedra Kristina gurgled.

Nedra looked at me. Her mother and father tried not to. The aunts folded and unfolded their hands. I repeated the prophecy: this very night God was going to bring perfection from those tiny lips.

The baby hiccuped.

And all at once Aunt Oretha, that wonderful, wise and gentle woman, threw back her head and laughed. "I don't know what kind of voice you're hearing, honey, but it sure isn't God's. Why He's just got better sense."

And with the sound of her laughter it was as if a clean, fresh wind blew through the muddle in my brain. Of course God had better sense than to desire a three-month-old infant to converse like an adult. That had been my own far-out interpretation of the Bible verse. Every bit of it had been me—the Christmas tree, still lying forlorn and frozen at the curb, the brainstorm about going out to Arizona. All a great big head trip.

"I'll make coffee," said Nedra. And no one in the family mentioned the scene again.

But the first thing I did when I got to the office on Monday was to shut myself in Pat Robertson's office and pour out the whole tale of error. "So much for prophecy," I summed up.

To my annoyance, instead of apologizing for his role in the whole debacle, Pat nodded as though this were a perfectly predictable turn of events. "I told you to experiment," he agreed. "And when you did, you got stung. Satan stepped in and nearly scared you off altogether, didn't he?"

Satan stepped in . . . The words didn't sound so much like a figure of speech as they once had.

"Don't you know Satan's the great counterfeiter?" Pat went on. "He can whisper the most plausible ideas you've ever heard right in your ear. And he's the slickest old Bible quoter there is."

"Then—then how do you know prophecy from a big lie?"

There were three ways, Pat said. Not just one of them, but all three together were the way God confirmed His word to us. "Satan may trump up one of them, or even two, but he's too chaotic a character to get all three working together."

The written word, Pat went on, was the first test. "Check every voice you hear against the Bible. Where in the Bible does it say, for instance, that you shouldn't have a Christmas tree?"

"I don't know where, exactly. The woman who called said the Bible said you shouldn't decorate trees. She said it was a heathen custom."

"Of course it was a heathen custom—to start with! Most customs were. Don't take anybody's word about what's in the Bible. Check it out for yourself."

Next, said Pat, test the prophecy in your own spirit. Bring everything you have to bear on it—experience, commonsense, your own past history, your inclinations. "Our spirit is to test the spirits, you know."

And finally, he said, when scripture and your own spirit agree, lay your proposed action before the body of Christ. "Not some guy you never met who calls up on the telephone. I'm talking about the recognized elders of the church, my friend. Recognized local leaders who will hear out your prophecy and give a mature judgement like it says in First Corinthians. Remember how—"

But I was no longer listening. Words like *elders* and *leaders* were banging around my head. Then—where was freedom? Where was the Spirit? Where were the things Nedra and I were looking for when we signed on for this Christian trip?

If I was going to have to start taking orders now, checking it out with some kind of committee everytime I wanted to sneeze, I might just as well be back in one of those narrow little churches I'd grown up in, with a list of rules ten miles long and everyone minding everyone else's business. The ones that picked my father to death with their gossiping and spying. No thanks. I wasn't going to listen to anyone but Jesus.

Those other two tests, though—your own inner witness and what the Bible had to say—they sounded okay. And six months later I had a chance to try them out.

It was a hot afternoon in July when I bumped into Pat in the hallway of CBN. In his hand he held a letter.

"Interesting, Scott," he said, handing me the letter as we passed.

Interesting indeed! Even as I read, my heart gave a little jump. The letter was from a man named Andy Andersen and it described a chain of FM stations in upstate New York. My eyes raced ahead. There were five stations, linked into a little network. An unusual network too, for they overlapped—and today FCC regulations would prohibit this. You could drive a car all the way from Buffalo, New York to Albany, New York and never be out of range of these overlapping stations.

And these facilities were for sale. They were currently owned by a telephone company, but a recent court decision required it to sell. Andersen wrote that he thought they could be bought for half a million dollars. "A good price," he said. A half-million-dollar bargain! I knew Pat and his associates had about zilch dollars in the bank.

I put the letter on Pat's desk. But I couldn't so easily get it out of my mind. I wondered if this was what it meant to have your spirit witness to a thing. I had often heard the phrase, "to get a burden" for something. That was exactly what it felt like. The sensation I felt in my heart for those five radio stations was like a weight. Heavy, but not unpleasant. The stations were my responsibility; I must pray for them.

Which is just what I did. Sometimes I prayed for half a million dollars, other times I prayed they wouldn't cost that much. Just, God, let there be some way we can bring those stations into the CBN network.

"Think of it, Nedra," I said one evening as we sat propped up on our mattress-bed with Nedra Kristina asleep between us. "Upstate New York. Dozens of colleges and universities. All those kids. And suddenly five radio stations are waiting to be bought. Just sitting behind a microphone we could talk to students at Cornell and Syracuse and Rochester and Rensselaer and Colgate. We could talk straight. We could let it all hang out. It would be something brand new."

"What does Pat say about it?" asked Nedra.

What Pat said, of course, every time we talked, was, "Where's the money going to come from?"

But then one day he had an idea: "Look, Scott," he said, "if the phone company is going to have to sell those stations for cash and then pay a tax on the transaction, why don't they give them away to CBN and claim a charitable deduction?"

We stood staring at each other. "It might work," I said. "It just might work."

By the end of the week Nedra and I *knew* it was going to work. Friday night we got a baby-sitter and went out to a little coffee house. While we were sitting there a young man came over to our table.

"You're Scott Ross, aren't you?"

"That's right. Do we know each other?"

"No. I saw an article about you in the *Pilot*."

So we sat around making small talk.

"Where are you from?" I asked.

"Upstate New York."

Nedra and I exchanged glances. We told him about the network of FM stations we were praying for.

"Oh, those stations," the young man said. "Sure I know them. I used to listen to them while I studied. Most of the students do, because they play background music. You know, not a lot of talk. Listen, if you got those stations you'd have a built-in audience."

"I still can't get over it," I said to Nedra next morning at breakfast. "What are the chances of running into that guy and his bringing up the business about students and those stations? I tell you, love, God's in this thing!"

Nedra buttered some toast. The words "Christmas tree" and "Arizona" were never spoken between us, but they had made both of us shy about proclaiming what God did or didn't want.

Check everything against the written word . . . The Bible was beside the teapot. What if I were to open it, just anywhere, and see if it confirmed this idea.

Feeling embarrassed because I wasn't sure it was okay to use the Bible this way, I flipped it open somewhere in the middle and stuck my finger on the page. My finger landed on Isaiah 55:12:

For ye shall go out with joy, and be led forth with peace; the mountains and the hills shall break forth before you into singing, and all the trees of the field shall clap their hands.

I read it again, scarcely believing it. "Oh, wow, Nedra. If this *is* God speaking to us, we're going to be going up there, you and I, and there's going to be singing and the whole place celebrating because of what's going on."

Nedra took the Bible from me and read the verse herself. "Are there really lots of hills and trees in upstate New York, Scott?"

"Nothing but."

She picked up Nedra Kristina from her wicker basket. "You've got a kooky daddy, honey." But as she said it she was dancing with the baby around the green metal table.

Monday I told Pat about the Isaiah verse. Pat was excited in his unflappable way. "I hear it, Scott," he said. "In fact, let's get on the morning show right now and tell people about this."

"We've made a definite proposal to the telephone company," Pat said into the microphone, and then laughed. "That is, we've asked them to *give* the stations to us. And now here comes this scripture which the Lord gives Scott. If we're hearing God correctly, the Rosses are to go forth and the very hills around Ithaca will sing. Will you pray with us right now for those stations?"

It was two days later that Pat was waiting outside the studio when I got to work.

"They've accepted, haven't they?" I said.

"They have!" For once Pat's cool was undone. "It's just a matter of the paperwork now. The stations are ours! When can you leave?" he ran on without a pause. "We can swing a twenty-five dollar raise for the higher cost of living up there."

I must have looked hesitant because he started telling me all over again what a great opportunity the stations were. "I know the money's not great, but if you got along on a hundred dollars a week here, you should be able to make it on a hundred and twenty-five up there."

But it wasn't the money. Just, somehow, I'd never really pictured what it would be like to pick up and move, baby and all, to some place we'd never laid eyes on, and now that the time was actually here I was scared.

But Pat had been right when he'd said that God's signposts, when they come, never come singly. Everything—but everything—suddenly pointed us away from Portsmouth. Even the townhouse where we'd been so comfortable, all at once wasn't comfortable any more.

It happened when some of Nedra's family came down for two weeks in August. Funny how no one had ever noticed their skin color before. Now we began to get comments from the neighbors.

"You know, Mr. Ross, it's not that *we* have any objection to these people, but I'm going to be selling my house soon, and you know what happens to real estate values when . . ."

Yeah. Anyhow, I believe the Lord let this happen as an added direction signal. Nedra and I had an easy time packing, since most of our furniture belonged to CBN anyhow. We'd sold Nedra's car to pay Nedra Kristina's hospital bills. We rented the smallest U-Haul truck available and took the highway north.

The needle of the Empire State Building rose out of the industrial fog of New Jersey as we approached New York City. I remembered the first time I'd seen that spire, a lonesome kid of sixteen, riding up to the observation tower to dream dreams of glory. Here I was, twelve years later, my worldly possessions not filling the back of a small U-Haul . . .

Ithaca is 250 miles northwest of New York. On September 1, 1968, Nedra and I pulled the truck to the crest of a hill overlooking the town. A fabulous world lay below us. Geologically, the land was glacier country. Huge ice fingers had gouged out the area, leaving long slender valleys which filled with water. Ithaca sat between two parallel ranges of hills, at the southern end of one of these deepwater lakes. Here and there already a scarlet tree announced the oncoming fall.

Our only contact in Ithaca was Andy Andersen, the man who had been running the station and acting as intermediary between the telephone company and Pat Robertson. We located Andy's house and got a big welcome. He and his wife Robin couldn't wait to drive us up to the transmitter.

What a site for a radio station! Chipmunks, woodchucks, a porcupine and a deer ran to cover as Andy's car crunched up the gravel road. Years ago some farmer had built himself a house way out here. The network had purchased the property and erected a transmitting tower in the back yard. The farmhouse was now studio and office, and to run both there was only a skeleton crew headed by Andy.

The Andersens insisted we stay with them until we could work out living arrangements of our own. And so began our search for a home, the search which—though we didn't suspect it at the time—was to lead to so much more.

Each day we pored over the real estate columns in the local paper. There were very few rentals, and what did exist was out of our range. Using the textbook rule of one-week's-pay-for-the-rent, we could spend $125 a month for housing. There was never anything near this price. Then one day Nedra said:

"Scott, look at this. Under MOBILE HOMES: 'Trailer for rent. $90.00.' And it's furnished!"

Andy looked at the address and nodded; the trailer was on the very road that led to the transmitter. That same afternoon we all drove out to take a look at it. The trailer sat catty-cornered on a lot next to an isolated farmhouse. It was small and tinny and I wondered how it would stand up to the deep freeze of Ithaca's sub-zero winter. But inside it was cozy and homelike. Twenty minutes later we signed a month-to-month rental agreement.

That night I phoned Pat to report progress. The plan was for me to stay at the transmitter until the beginning of 1969 when the Christian programming could begin.

"That's over three months off," Pat said. "You won't have anything to do except play records. Know what I suggest you do with your time, Scott? Read the Bible. What an opportunity! Wish I had it myself."

And that's exactly what I did. For three months, for twelve hours a day, from six in the morning until six in the evening, I played background music, breaking in occasionally to read the news. But basically, I knew, I'd been given this time to find out what God said in His Word.

During this time too I settled on the kind of program I wanted once CBN officially took over the stations. I got out a map of New York state and drew circles around the five outlets—Ithaca, Syracuse, Schenectady, Rochester, Buffalo—each circle representing the FM range. It was true that you could drive across the whole state and never lose the voice of CBN-Northeast.

My dream was to reach my kind of people with a contemporary

sound. Instead of the usual back-to-back preaching of most Christian radio stations, ours would have varied programming. Mine would be the evening show, and I'd call it *Tell It Like It is*. In between good records people could call in to talk about their problems; I knew from my experience in Portsmouth that there was no better setting for a natural lead-in to Jesus. The show would be reaching into bars and automobiles and dorms and drug-scene parties: the "market place" where my kind of people hung out, hungry and thirsty for something they couldn't define.

And afterwards, when they found the answer—what then? The ones Jesus would call, the ones He would heal: where would they go? To some red brick church-on-the-corner, dressed, like the man said, in "appropriate attire"?

I didn't have any answers to that one. I wasn't sure anybody did.

7

And all the while the weather grew colder. The colors outside the studio window were so brilliant they almost hurt my eyes. Then the leaves fell, the hard freeze came, and finally there was snow.

And more snow.

Many days I took Nedra and Nedra Kristina with me to the transmitter, for we were all having problems with lonesomeness. We'd sit at the farmhouse windows watching the snow build up, waiting for the plow to come through. One day when we got back to our little mobile home, the thermometer outside read 20 degrees below zero.

We had no way of knowing that the winter weather itself was one of the ways God would lead us in His direction.

At last, all the paperwork was complete. The Christian Broadcasting Network was in full possession of the five stations interlocking across the top of New York State. Pat Robertson flew up from Portsmouth for the official opening of CBN-Northeast. A friend of Pat's, Harald Bredesen, was supposed to join us too, but Harald got mixed up and flew to Utica, instead of Ithaca.

"Typical," said Pat. "But he'll probably end up discovering that the Spirit sent him to Utica for a special reason."

Still, we were quite a crowd who gathered to launch the new outlets in prayer: Pat, Nedra and myself, Andy Andersen who was to be general manager of the stations for CBN, Robin Andersen, the guys who were to handle the morning and afternoon programming, a secretary, technical staff. Together we claimed the airwaves for the Lord, asking that from the very first day miracles would be performed in these hills and valleys.

January 1, 1969, was our first full day of broadcasting. My show ran from seven P.M. till midnight, Monday through Saturday. That first night, to my surprise, I found myself talking about Nedra Kristina's healing—how Dr. Roe had called her his "miracle" baby. I kept wondering why I was telling this now—I certainly hadn't planned to. I kept getting the feeling I was talking not just into the air, but straight to some particular person.

It was several weeks before I heard the other side of the story.

A few miles outside of Ithaca, in a little town with the improbable name of Freeville, lived a widow named Peg Hardesty. Peg's home was a brown-shingle farmhouse sitting close up to the road next to a tumble-down barn.

For thirteen years Peg Hardesty had been crippled by arthritis, so painful she couldn't even lift herself out of bed in the morning, but had to roll down onto the floor, then struggle to her knees and her feet. She got through the day on large doses of Darvon and Valium.

It happened that the very first night we were on the air Peg had trouble with her AM radio: not a single station would come in. So she switched to FM and twirled the dial, looking for music. Suddenly to her surprise she caught the word "Jesus." Some man seemed to be talking about religion. He was saying that Jesus had come to set people free and to heal. "We saw this happen in our own family. When our little daughter, Nedra Kristina, was born . . ." As Peg lay on her couch, listening, a great peace flooded her entire body. The next morning she sat up; then stood. She walked about the house with no desire to take the usual drugs.

The pain was gone.

Just like that.

At first, although she was a Christian and believed theoretically in God's power to heal, Peg couldn't accept what had happened to her: people just didn't get over arthritis with a snap of the finger. All that day, and the next, and the next, she gingerly went about her house and farm chores, fully expecting the crippling pain to come back.

It never did.

But though, as I say, we didn't know this story, we were hearing others like it. We started getting fantastic letters the very first week. People were finding Jesus, or breaking destructive habits, or receiving the Baptism in the Holy Spirit, all while listening to the show. It seemed like every prayer we'd ever made for these stations was being answered. Not just among young people, either. An elderly man wrote that cataracts on both eyes had simply "dissolved" one night as he listened to a college girl phoning in to accept Jesus. A marriage in Elmira was headed back from divorce. A Cornell professor overcame a problem with jealousy.

And it wasn't only Christians who were tuning us in. We really were reaching out to all kinds of scenes. People would call up from bars and taverns, talk to us and ask for prayers. Students would call in the middle of a wild party and come to the Lord. Right on the air.

I remember one night while I was chatting about how we'd seen a deer that morning from the trailer window, a long distance call came through. A young man's voice said, "This is Bob Whyley. I'm a college student in Albany."

Bob Whyley must have racked up a huge telephone bill that night because we talked for an hour and a half. He asked some heavy questions: why did I think the Bible was inspired, did I really believe prophets could foretell the future, what made me think that Jesus was God? As often happened, we stayed on the air past our scheduled sign-off time of midnight, and about 12:30 that morning I suddenly knew that I should ask Bob outright if he would like to know the Lord.

"Yes," Bob said. As quick as that.

We prayed together and Bob accepted the Lord then and there, over the air. When he hung up at last, I was too exhilarated to sign off. I kept playing records and every few minutes Bob would call back.

"Man, I can't understand what's happening. It's like no trip I've ever been on!"

And a few minutes later: "Scott, I've just got to sing. Why didn't someone tell me about this before!" It was three o'clock that morning before we went off the air. This is what I had been wanting to do! Reach out with radio to where the young people were and talk to them straight.

Only—with Bob as with all the other people I knew by voice only—I had this unanswered question. What next? Where was Bob supposed to go now, to be fed and encouraged and get all the other things a new-born Christian needs? How I wished there was some place guys like Bob could be *culturally* comfortable while they grew up in the Lord. After all, the people in the red brick churches did exactly that: they were culturally right at home as they worshipped God. But their way of talking and dressing and living would be as off-putting to Bob Whyley as his would be to them.

At the station we were having trouble in this same department. Listeners were calling up in varying degrees of culture shock. "Did Jesus Christ listen to rock and roll records?" one man demanded. I wanted to remind him that Jesus didn't call people on the telephone, either, but you know—what's the use. Another time a lady sent in a donation of a hundred dollars with the stipulation that we never again play "that record about dancing." (Robert Edwin's beautiful song, *Lord of the Dance.*) It was Portsmouth all over again, except that this time we were able to send back the money and go on playing the music. *Tell It Like It Is,* we explained to these people, was aimed from the start at non-committed young adults—especially the non-church-going college student.

Still, we wished there was a way for us to follow through better.

With Bob Whyley we were lucky. We couldn't go to him, but he came to us.

It happened one night after we'd mentioned on the air that

CBN-Northeast was looking for a newscaster. Once more the long distance call from Albany.

"Hi, Bob! How's it going?"

"Cloud nine, man." But Bob had something else on his mind. "I hear you need a newsman," he went on. "Did I ever tell you I'm studying radio?"

Right away, I suspected we'd be seeing more of Bob Whyley. "Come on out and we'll give you an audition."

The following Saturday Bob drove from Albany to Ithaca. We gave him a news report to read and he was really good. He made arrangements to take a leave of absence from college as soon as the current semester was over. And soon we were able to report on the air, "Do you remember, folks, how we've been praying for a newsman? Well, we've found him. I'll turn the microphone over to him now. Here is the Christian Broadcasting Network's most recent employee, newsman Bob Whyley."

The weather was setting all sorts of for-the-date records. If we'd been in a house with good insulation and a good furnace, it might almost have been fun. But living in that little trailer with the thermometer out the window now reading minus 25—in no way could this be called fun.

Nedra Kristina was walking now—running was more like it, the precipitous, headlong charge of a 16-month-old—but since outside was nothing but snowdrifts and sub-zero gales, her space for exploring was the few narrow feet between the bed and the kitchen table. In addition, the erratic temperature of the little trailer affected her bronchial tubes, which doctors had warned us were unusually narrow. Especially when she lay down we would hear her struggling for breath, crying out in fear when no air came. Many night when I came home from the studio in the small, dark hours, slithering and sliding over the ice-glazed snow, I would find Nedra rocking the sobbing little girl in her arms, every blanket in the place wrapped around the two of them.

One morning Nedra poked me awake just after dawn. I could see our breath hanging above the bed. "Listen," she said. "It's awfully quiet." I listened, but couldn't hear the hum, buzz, clink of the oil burner.

"Oh, oh," I said.

I got up and checked the furnace. Sure enough, no heat. Even the inside thermometer read below freezing. If it went any lower the pipes would break.

"Nedra, I don't know what to do. I'm no furnace man."

Nedra leaned out of bed, lifted the baby from her crib, and tucked her beneath our covers. "When in doubt, kick," Nedra said.

I kicked but nothing happened.

"When still in doubt, pray," Nedra said.

"Oh come on, Nedra."

"No, you come on; I'm serious. Nedra Kristina's cheeks are like ice."

And so I laid hands on the oil burner and prayed very simply, "Lord Jesus, I know You don't want us to freeze. Please make this furnace go."

Of course nothing happened. I was starting back for the comparative warmth of bed when, ". . . wwhrr, wwhrr," that old burner started up.

Nedra and I spent quite a while that morning praising God.

Still, this was no way to be taking care of a baby.

"Scott," Nedra said to me one morning as she turned on the stove burners to try to get a bit of extra warmth, "the Andersens said we could stay at their place anytime it got too cold here. I think that time has come."

So Nedra and the baby moved in with Robin and Andy—and a good thing.

It was a few nights later that I slid down the hill from the radio station, parked the car beside the trailer, opened the door and knew that we had spent our last night in that little home.

While I had been at the studio the furnace had gone off again, and this time the pipes had broken for sure. Cascades of ice tumbled from the bathroom and the kitchen. Nedra Kristina's toys were frozen solid onto the floor. I slithered and skidded into the bedroom only long enough to pick up a pair of pajamas and a toothbrush.

And even in this, God was at work.

But at the time it only seemed hairy. All three of us were now living in a single room at the Andersens'.

"You should have seen it, folks," I grumbled over the air. I told about the broken pipes and the ice-skating rink inside the trailer and Nedra Kristina's cough that was no better even in the Andersens' warm house. "Now the Andersens aren't getting any sleep either. Please join us in praying for a place of our own. If the Lord can start up a rusty old oil burner, He can find us an apartment."

But several weeks went by and nothing turned up. We did have one rather humorous reply to our appeals over the air. A lady called up from a place called Freeville—Peg Hardesty she said her name was—and told us a long story about being healed from arthritis the very first day we were on the air. "You mentioned you were looking for a place to live," she continued. "There's a barn here on my place."

"A barn?"

"Yes. A great big one."

"Full of pigs and horses and cows and things?"

"Just the four cows and a pony. And the chickens, of course."

"Well, ah, Mrs. Hardesty—what was your thought?"

There was silence over the telephone. Then a half-embarrassed laugh. "You know, I don't have the slightest idea! It doesn't make any sense, does it? I only know every time you've mentioned needing a home, I've had this incredible nudging: *Tell him about the barn.* So finally I did."

"Well, ah—thank you very much, Mrs. Hardesty. But I don't really know what we'd do with a barn. It must be as cold inside those things as out."

"Pretty near. But—are you sure you don't want to just come out and take a look?"

And so, more to get her off the phone than anything else, I said great. Some day when Nedra and I were out toward Freeville we would drop in to see her barn. You know, radio stations get all kinds of crazy calls.

But it was almost immediately after this one that we did in fact find an apartment. It was almost as if we had needed to keep hunting, needed to keep mentioning it over the air, until Peg Hardesty made that call. Then all at once the perfect place turned up. It was a duplex apartment in a big white frame house on Elm Street near downtown Ithaca. Upstairs were two bedrooms and a bath, downstairs a large living room, a dining room, a den—even a (ha! ha!) maid's room off the kitchen. After the narrow confines of a trailer and a single room it seemed to us a palace—and to Nedra Kristina a whole continent to explore.

"Why do I keep thinking about that crazy woman with the barn?" I asked Nedra one day as I balanced a board across some bricks to make us a bookcase. "Last night I even dreamed about barns."

"Maybe you're supposed to go out and look at it like you said you would," Nedra said. "I'd love to take a drive."

So that afternoon we bundled up little Nedra, got into the second-hand Karman-Ghia which we had recently purchased, and headed out of town. From the map, Freeville appeared to be about ten miles east of Ithaca. We drove out the four-lane highway overlooking the lake. Beyond the airport Route 13 narrowed. Huge piles of snow banked the sides of the road. It was bitter cold; wind blasted off the tops of the banks and whirled them across the highway. About ten miles out we passed a sign saying Kirk Road.

"Weel now, lassie," I said in my best Scottish brogue. "Kir-rk Road. That means 'Church Road.' A bonnie fair-r-r portent."

Sure enough, just beyond this road was a mailbox with the name "Hardesty." I wanted to keep right on going. The farmyard was filled with derelict tractors and rusting bits of machinery, and beside the road was an enormous flimsy-looking hulk of a barn, only here and there showing traces of an ancient coat of red paint. The driveway down to the farmhouse was sheeted with ice.

"We'd never get back out of there," I said to Nedra.

"Oh come on, Scott. We're here now."

So I inched down to the side of the house. We got out of the car and dashed through the wind and snow up to the porch. I rapped on the glass door-pane and the next minute was looking into a pleasant round face.

In fact Peg Hardesty's face was one big smile. She looked about 50, stocky, fair-haired. And barefoot.

"You must be that fellow from the radio station," she said.

"That's right. This is my wife Nedra, Mrs. Hardesty."

"Come inside where it's warm. And call me Peg."

She took us into the principal room of the house: the kitchen. Peg lived in the downstairs of the house only; the upstairs, she explained, was rented out. The kitchen was warm, bright and spotless.

"How's the arthritis?" Nedra said.

Peg held out her hands and flexed her fingers. "No crippling. No pain. And that's not the only thing. When you started talking about the Baptism in the Holy Spirit on your show, I asked the Lord to baptize me too. And you know, He did!"

So this was the explanation of Peg's sparkle. I wondered how many other stories, parallel to hers, were being repeated in isolated farmhouses throughout New York State.

"Would you like to see the barn?" she asked after a while.

"Sure," I said untruthfully.

Peg put on a coat, pulled rubber boots over her bare feet and headed across the snowy yard, the three of us following. Huge snowdrifts lay up against the weathered barnside, and I discovered immediately why barns have sliding doors in this part of the world. Peg hauled one of the doors aside and we stepped through. If anything it was colder inside the place than out. It was also dark. A 25-watt bulb, further dulled by cobwebs, gleamed wanly from the ceiling high above. A growl greeted us and Peg stooped to pat a white shadow against the wall.

"This is Niki," she said. "He's a Samoyede. A Siberian sled dog. I have to keep him chained or he gets the chickens."

I didn't say anything. I was having a typical city-boy's reaction to the smells of a barn. Peg led us through a door to where some cows were munching in their stanchions. A cat scurried away and Nedra Kristina wanted to run after him, but I couldn't set her down in this muck. I kept wiping my feet to get the smell off.

"This your first time in a barn, Scott?" Peg asked.

"Does it show that bad?"

Peg took us through some more doors. There was some rickety old furniture, stacks of boards, mattresses, pipes, an old piano. These people must have been saving stuff all their lives, I thought. We climbed up into a granary which was covered with old license plates and metal Coke signs to keep mice out.

And then, suddenly, at the top of another ladder, we were in the part of the barn where the hay was stored.

My heart gave a strange little leap. What was there about this dim dusty loft with pigeons strutting along the beams and a wintery sun straggling through the cracks in the roof, that should set my pulse pounding? I stood there a moment on the top rung of the ladder, struggling with the feeling that I'd seen this all before.

But that was impossible. For the first time since we'd entered the barn there was light enough, up here, to read my watch. "We have to head back," I called down to Nedra. I had to be at the station at 4:00 each afternoon to go on the air by 7:00.

"Well, let me give you a little milk before you go," Peg said. We picked our way out of the littered barn, sliding the doors shut on the smells and the clucking of chickens. Back in the kitchen Peg gave us a gallon of ice cold milk which we accepted gratefully. I set the jug on the floor of the car as Nedra settled Nedra Kristina on her lap. That driveway was just as treacherous to get out of as it had looked. At last when the highway was clear I got a running start and gunned it up the little rise.

We made it onto the road but the jug toppled over and all the way home a small lake of milk was sloshing over our shoes. With rags and towels we mopped it up as best we could, but it was weeks before we got the sour smell out of the automobile.

All in all, then, the visit to the barn was something short of a pleasure.

Which made it all the more difficult to explain what happened next.

In late March I flew out to Minneapolis to give a speech; Nedra and I were depending more and more on honoraria from speeches like this. As the plane left Ithaca airport, I looked down at Route 13. And there, like a doll set, was the Hardesty farm. I could see the crazy old barn, Peg's awkward driveway, her house. I could see a square-shaped cattle pond out back and the boundaries of the farm outlined by fence rows.

And as I looked I had the incredible impression of God's voice in some inner ear. It was as if the Lord were saying to me that this was His barn. In spite of the fact that it was filled with muck and smells and abandoned, rusting relics, this was His place and He was going to use it.

I tried to shake off the idea. It was too far-out.

"Lord, is this my head, or is this really You?"

In answer I received a crisp impression:

I want you to go out to the barn again.

So in sheer obedience, after work a few nights after my return from Minneapolis, I drove out to the Hardesty place again. I parked the car and slid open the big door, grateful for the chain which held Niki, and hoping his ruckus wouldn't have Peg phoning the police. I stood just inside the door, trying to adjust my eyes to the gloom. It was just as I remembered it—cows and dirt and accumulated trash. So how to explain what was happening inside me? For instead of seeing the barn as an ugly old place held together with baling wire and license plates, I was seeing it somehow with eyes of love. It was almost as though Jesus Himself were showing it to me.

Scott, you're beginning to get it. Keep looking. I want you to learn to see things the way I do, not as they are, but as they can be. I want you to see the shimmering beauty that is hiding in dirty old barns—and in men—waiting only to be released.

Not as they are . . . I wandered further into the barn, feeling beneath my feet not these creaking boards and rotting straw piles, but strong and holy ground.

I climbed the ladder to the loft, moonlight sifting through the splintered roof. And then I remembered where I had seen this room before. On the bus. This was the very place I'd seen in my vision as the bus crawled up Eighth Avenue nearly two years ago! I swallowed to keep down the lump in my throat. This big square room, those beams up there, that high peaked ceiling, every detail exactly as I had seen it. Only—in the vision the room had been packed with young people, and there'd been a band where now there was only a decaying pile of hay. And there'd been singing and laughter and joyful faces and a lot of other things that made no sense at all in this silent old loft on Route 13.

8

Over the next several weeks I developed a strange routine. I would get home from the radio station at about two o'clock in the morning, fall into bed for a few hours' sleep, be up for breakfast, play with Nedra Kristina, and then . . . head out to the barn and start heaving old mattresses out into the yard.

The only thing I didn't know was what I was doing it for. Sometimes I talked about my puzzlement on the air. "Now I want to ask you—what is there about that drafty old barn that makes me take the long drive out to Peg Hardesty's every day?"

When I got to the cow stalls I had to forget about breakfast. As I shoveled deeper into the rotting manure heaps, the acrid fumes made my nose sting, my eyes weep. Peg came out one morning to find me retching, around behind the tractor shed.

"You know, Scott," she said gently, "Jesus was born in a stable."

I picked up the shovel and went back to work.

At first I asked Peg's permission for anything I wanted to do. But after a while she said, "Now Scott, you do what you want with this barn. You don't have to keep coming to me."

I doubt that she would have been quite so relaxed if she had foreseen the influx of people who began to appear. After I talked about the barn on the air, phone calls would come in from local students: "Could we come out and give you a hand?"

Pretty soon students from Ithaca and Cornell, even as far away as Syracuse, began showing up. As each new car or motorcycle crunched down her gravel driveway, I'd see Peg's round face appear in her kitchen window. They came in their levis and Nehru shirts and granny glasses, and they came to work. Down came the Coca-Cola signs, the license plates, the cobwebs. Out went the rotten boards and the mail order catalogues.

The great part was, these were the very people I wanted most to talk to. I remembered the old shyness I had felt down in Bookmasters in New York, when I tried to talk about Jesus to people like these. Now it came naturally, in terms of the work we were doing. For instance one day a guy came to me carrying a rusty car wheel.

"What should I do with this, Scott?"

I looked at it: the wheel was bent and warped and would never hold a tire. I told him to throw it out, and while I was at it told him about the useless stuff God was helping me chuck out of my life as well.

Sometimes the encounters weren't so pleasant. One time as I came into the barn a Cornell student saw me, quickly took something out of his mouth and flipped it out the door. He grabbed a broom and began sweeping like crazy, but heavy on the air was the sour-sweet smell of marijuana.

I didn't say anything at the time. But the rest of the morning I found myself brooding over it. I couldn't very well take a holier-than-thou attitude, the way I'd used drugs. Still, a bust was the last thing we needed. So in the end I talked to the guy.

"Look," I said, "what you do about grass is up to you. But you can't smoke it here. It's illegal—you could get the whole lot of us arrested."

I expected an argument. To my surprise the guy almost seemed to welcome my stand.

"Okay, man. That's cool. It's your roof."

I was so relieved at the way he took it that it wasn't till later, driving home, that I realized what he'd said. *My* roof? That was a laugh. The barn wasn't *my* place, it was just—well, I didn't know what it was, except I sure didn't want to be saddled with it.

That was the way things happened, at the barn. They were done before you knew what was going on. One morning in May I was outside nailing down some loose boards so they wouldn't flap every time the wind blew, when this hitchhiker comes walking along Route 13 with a pack on his back.

"Hi."

"Hi."

Soon we were talking. His name was Philip. Where was he from? Chicago. What was he into? Nothing, he was just back from Vietnam; what were we into? Jesus. Yeah? That's far out. Pretty soon Philip was nailing boards alongside me.

The thing is that at the end of the day Philip unrolled his sleeping bag and sacked out in the hayloft. I didn't know about it till I got there the next day, and of course it was okay. It was just, you know, I didn't want to end up with a hotel.

We didn't even have a name for the barn. I still talked about it occasionally on the evening show: "Well, I went out to that old barn at Peg Hardesty's on Route 13 today, and . . ." Listeners sent in suggestions for names, but nothing seemed right.

Then one day Nedra and Nedra Kristina and I were all out there. In spite of the fact that the weather had been warm for weeks, Nedra Kristina's bronchitis was no better. Some nights she and Nedra got no sleep at all, and then were too tired next day to do anything but drag around the apartment. But that day they were out there, and so was Bob Whyley, and Philip the Vietnam veteran who was still sleeping in the loft, and maybe a dozen college kids including a girl named Mia Hansen who had made a commitment to Jesus as the result of the radio show. A bunch of us were standing out by the highway admiring the now battened-down walls.

"You know," said Nedra, "this place really and truly needs a name."

"If it's Jesus' place," said Bob, "maybe we ought to ask *Him* for a name." New Christians always kept the rest of us on our toes.

So right there beside the road, we bowed our heads. "Lord," I said, "help us to welcome anybody who comes to this barn. Just let it be one great love-in for Jesus."

Philip pounded me on the back. "That's it!"

"That's what?"

"Love Inn!" he said. "A love-in for Jesus. Don't you get it? This is Love Inn!"

Well we all went wild. We shouted and cheered till we created a little traffic jam from drivers slowing down to stare. Mia Hansen ran for a paint can. L-O-V-E I-N-N, she printed across the huge sliding doors. A great love-in, that was what our funky old barn was. A place where Jesus' love was to be found.

I'd read a lot in the Bible about names, how giving a name changes things, but I'd never watched it happen till now. Originally the scuttlebutt in Ithaca was that a bunch of hippies had taken over the barn for drug and sex orgies. But after Mia painted the name on the doors, a reporter from the local newspaper came out, took photographs, and wrote a story on us. She did a good job explaining what we were trying to do. Word got around: there was a love fest going on at Peg Hardesty's, all right, but it was some kind of religious love.

Our own thinking was strangely clarified too. One warm June day I was alone in an old storeroom that had once been piled floor to ceiling with junk. The stuff was mostly gone now, piled outside waiting to be carted away. The room was nearly empty— and then I stared. Against the blank wall I "saw" a row of bookcases filled with books. In another wall was a window, where certainly there hadn't been one a minute before, a window with a kind of colored glass effect. Here was a sofa, over there some chairs. There was even a carpet on the floor, and I saw to my surprise that it was made up of bits of different colors, like Joseph's coat.

As I stared, it was an empty storeroom again. But I knew without a doubt that I had "seen" the library and bookstore that would one day occupy this space. It was the experience on the bus all over again—as though giving the barn a name had opened the way for God to show me more of His plan for it.

I stepped out of the storeroom and walked slowly through the milking barn. The animals had been outside since early spring; floor and walls were scrubbed and disinfected. But where in actuality were concrete cow stanchions, I "saw" tables and benches. One end of this section was a large well-equipped kitchen. Above my head the barn beams had been stripped of whitewash and glowed a deep natural brown. Against the rear wall—and now I really blinked—was a huge fireplace with a blazing fire in it.

I climbed the ladder to the haymow. Only it wasn't a ladder any more, but a broad solid staircase: I saw how it utilized a minimum of space. And the haymow was now a stage. The silo was a prayer room. Beneath that, the pony stalls had been turned into sleeping rooms . . .

"Wait a minute!" I said out loud. "People will be sleeping here *permanently?*" My work was in radio. I was a disc jockey; I wasn't going to turn nursemaid to a bunch of strung-out kids.

And at that moment the unrolling vision ceased.

Nedra was fascinated when I told her what I'd seen; she insisted on hearing every detail. "If it really was a look into the future, Scott, it's clear that the Lord only showed you as much as you were ready for. The minute you got frightened, He stopped."

"Maybe. Maybe it wasn't a true vision at all. Maybe it was just my head."

But a few days later I told Peg about it, including the part about the dormitory in the pony stalls. We were sitting in her kitchen drinking iced tea. Even as I spoke a girl wandered out of the barn dropping a gum wrapper on the ground behind her. Peg bit her lip. I knew how she felt. It was one thing to rap with people over the telephone, another to have to live with them.

"It scares me too, Peg." But . . . if the vision had come from God? "If you're willing to trust this thing for a while, Peg, I certainly am."

"I'm willing, Scott."

A couple of days later Peg said she wanted to make a legal gift to us of the barn and the land immediately around it. We formed a non-profit corporation for the purpose, Jesus People, Inc. And with the signing of these papers we stepped over a threshold.

One part of the vision I had no trouble at all with. The old haymow was to be a theater—a place where people could come to perform and listen to the best in contemporary Christian music. After all, that was the scene God had originally shown me, nearly three years ago.

There was only one problem. Right in the center of what would be the seating area was the huge post that held up the roof. Leave it there and you couldn't see the stage, take it away and the roof would fall down. "Lord," I said as I stood there in the big twilit loft, "if this really is Your idea, You'll have to show me what to do about that post."

Instantly into my head came these instructions:

"That post is supporting a crossbeam. Get two smaller posts, six by six inches thick, and place them at either end of the crossbeam. Run braces like V's from the crossbeam to the roof. Then cut out the center post."

I stood staring up at the beam and the roof far over my head. I knew nothing whatsoever about construction, yet these directions had come with such authority.

The only thing to do was to check them out with an expert. Through Peg I got in touch with the best local carpenter, who one day drove out to the barn to stand with his hands in his overall pockets, looking up at the crossbeam and the center post while I explained what I was proposing.

"Do you think it would work?" I asked anxiously.

The carpenter pressed his lips together and walked from one side of the loft to the other, squinting up at the roof. Obviously he was not going to part with a word that was not absolutely necessary. Finally he gave one short nod.

"Yup," he said.

Still, it was a tense moment for me when, the six-by-sixes and counter-braces in place, we started sawing that tremendous center post through, top and bottom. At last, holding my breath, I picked up a sledge hammer and hit the bottom of the post until it crashed to the floor. Pigeons clattered into the air and dust rose in clouds, but the roof never shivered.

"Scott," said Peg one day in July as she showed me how to stake the beans in the garden we had put in behind her house, "where's Debbie going to sleep?"

I glanced down to the far end of the garden where Debbie Richardson was running about, generally getting in the way of the lettuce weeders. She'd arrived that morning from Roanoke, Virginia, and hadn't sat down or stopped talking since.

"Because she won't be going back to a college dorm tonight like the summer school girls," Peg pointed out. "And she can't very well sleep in the barn."

Ten or a dozen guys would be sleeping out there any night now in vacation time. No, Debbie couldn't stay in the barn.

Debbie Richardson was an eighteen-year-old time bomb who'd attended a talk I'd given recently down in Roanoke. As I spoke, she'd "known" that she was to come to Love Inn. And here she was: all energy and skinny arms and legs. Peg was looking at me, waiting for an answer.

"Ah . . . maybe she could stay with you, Peg?"

And that, I should have known, was a recipe for disaster.

Something else had happened in Roanoke, something I'd shared so far with no one but Nedra. I'd gone down there worried, as I was increasingly, by problems at the radio station. Every week now we were getting complaints from older listeners about the type of music I was playing on the evening show. Some of the calls and letters came to me, but Andy Andersen as station manager got most of them—recently he'd begun hinting that I should change the program's approach. Without ever intending to, I'd suddenly found myself describing all this to the audience in Roanoke.

"The trouble is," I said, *"Tell It Like It Is* goes out over Christian stations, and Christian audiences have come to expect only certain kinds of programs. One day I'm going to do a show that's aimed at regular commercial radio—the big rock stations. The music will be good enough to compete with the best, but the lyrics and the talk segment will be Christian. Then you'll really be out in the market place."

If the Roanoke audience had been surprised at this outburst, I'd been flabbergasted. I hadn't known I was thinking along these lines at all. And yet there was the idea, full blown and complete in my head. Was this Pat Robertson's "prophecy," even though the language was so ordinary? Ever since the Roanoke trip I'd been puzzling over it.

Meanwhile, with the hayloft-stage completed and the staircase in, we began holding "musical weekends" which soon started attracting people from a hundred miles away and more. I'd prerecord the radio show, Nedra would line up a sitter, and we'd drive out to the barn together. Many an evening I would look around the loft and see the very scene God had showed me on an Eighth Avenue bus. The room packed with young people, swaying, shouting, clapping their approval, while from the stage came the incredible sounds of a new kind of worship—not just Jesus rock, but something freer, fresher, totally reverent and totally today.

Among the young musicians who began to congregate at Love Inn as word got out, a few stayed on after the weekends, moving into the spare rooms at Peg's, becoming a regular part of Love Inn. Some of them were also mature Christians, so that Nedra, Peg and I got some help with the kids who stayed on after the concerts, as some always did—often for days—to learn more about Jesus.

Other parts of the barn-to-be that I had seen that June day were becoming a reality too. Some of the transformation we helped along ourselves, like renting sand blasting equipment to get the whitewashed ceiling downstairs back to its natural wood.

Other developments were harder to explain. One day we had a

visitor to the barn who told me he had a carpet store in Ithaca. He asked if we could use a load of discontinued rug samples. I went out to his truck to see what he was talking about. There, neatly stacked, were hundreds of squares of broadloom, the kind rug salesmen take with them on calls to customers.

"Pretty," I said. "But how would we ever use such small pieces?"

"Here, I'll show you," he said.

He carried an armload of the rug squares into the old storeroom which already had a few books in it, the start of our library. The guy dropped the samples on the floor, then knelt down and arranged them in an interesting pattern. "All you do," he said, "is glue these to a plywood base, and presto, you have a rug."

I didn't answer—but not because I didn't go for the idea. For at my feet lay the many-colored Joseph's Coat of a rug I had "seen" back in June in this very room.

And meanwhile, in the farmhouse, the relationship between Peg and Debbie was building to a blow-up. Almost every time I drove out to the barn Debbie would meet me in the driveway with some new tale of woe. Peg was a slave-driver, she said, who cared more about her stupid old house than letting Debbie pray or read the Bible or talk with the kids over at the barn. Peg, when I asked her about it, said she didn't feel that picking one's clothes off the floor and cleaning up after one's own meals constituted forced servitude.

Most of the time my sympathies were with Debbie because I could see that she was trying, really trying. Like the time she decided in a burst of good will to scrub the bathroom walls. That day, both of them met me in tears.

"My brand new tile!" wailed Peg. "I saved six years to put new tile in there!"

It seemed that the new tile was plastic and Debbie, instead of asking, had used cleansing powder on it and scratched it. I put my arm around Debbie and blew up at Peg. Wasn't Debbie's gesture of love more important than the precious bathroom tile? I mean, God was interested in people, not things.

One addition to the Love Inn cast Peg welcomed with open arms. One Saturday when I drove out there things seemed—I don't know—better organized than usual. A group was laying pipes for the kitchen we needed now in the barn, another group was spreading gravel in the new parking area.

I parked next to a blue pickup and walked into Peg's kitchen.

"Hi, Scott," Peg said. "Remember how we've been needing a supervisor? Well, he's out in the barn right now."

"Yeah? Who's that?"

"His name's Ken," she said. "Ken Spafard."

The night before, she told me, she'd heard Niki barking and looked out to see this blue truck pull into the drive. A man and a young boy got out and came to the door. The man introduced himself and his son Eddie, and asked if they could camp out and help us a bit. He said he was in the construction line.

"If you want to know the truth," Peg said, "it's good to see a face around here that's older than twenty-two."

I went to the barn. There was Ken Spafard showing two young men how to hold a saw. I took his roughened hand and introduced myself to him and his boy Eddie.

"Do you need anything built?" Ken Spafard asked

"We sure do. We need some eating tables."

So Ken went to work turning the old cow stalls into a dining area. As he sawed and hammered he told us that his wife Jean had cancer. Young Eddie was at the ten-year-old noisy stage; on weekends Ken had to find ways to keep him out of the house so Jean could rest. That night the two slept in the back of Ken's truck. When they left, Sunday afternoon, they promised to return.

At first Ken and Eddie came out to Love Inn only for an occasional weekend. But after Jean died, Ken and Eddie moved in, setting themselves up in a little shed out back of the barn. When Ken wasn't working on a job of his own, he was showing us how to shellac the now bare-wood ceiling beams, or helping us build a stable out back of Peg's where we could put the animals next winter.

It was fun watching Ken change. He came from a church that

reminded me of the dour, sad faced church I'd attended as a child in Glasgow. Now, working every day around young people, many of them brand new Spirit-baptized Christians, he began to absorb a little of the joy that permeated the place. Even as he struggled with grief for his wife, I could see a new aliveness appear in his eyes. At first I thought I must be imagining it, but as time went on there could be no doubt: Ken was letting his sideburns grow.

A long weepy phone call from Debbie had interrupted my morning Bible reading. Peg was still picking on her; Peg was the meanest person she'd ever known. I got her calmed down with a promise to speak to Peg when I got there later in the morning, and turned back to my reading in the sixth chapter of Ephesians.

Children, obey your parents in the Lord: for this is right.

These words which I had read with no special attention a few moments earlier, now seemed to burn and glitter on the page. Was Peg in some sense Debbie's "parent" in this situation? Were we— much as I tried to avoid the thought—were we becoming something more than just a random grouping of individuals, each going his own way? Were we, whether we wanted to or not, entering into some kind of deep, lasting relationship with one another?

I looked again at the Bible in my lap. "Obey" was such a harsh, old-fashioned word, out of place in today's world. Why then did this verse shine like gold upon the page, as though the key to an impossible situation had been placed suddenly in my hands.

Out at the farmhouse I could tell that Peg too had been in tears this morning.

"Is it Debbie, Peg?" I asked.

Peg was silent.

"Where is she?"

"She's out riding the pony."

"But I thought you asked her yesterday to help you do the account books this morning."

"Well, she didn't do it, Scott, she's out riding."

Just at that moment through the kitchen window I saw Debbie going into the new stable with the pony. I waited but she did not come out. So I walked up to the stable, and there was Deb leaning over the gate to the pony's stall, feeding him lumps of sugar.

At that instant a strange thing happened. I felt as if I *had* to speak to Debbie, letting the Lord use my lips. "I have a message for you, Deb," I told her, and then remembering the Portsmouth "prophecies," told her she would have to weigh for herself whether or not it came from the Lord:

"Debbie, you came here because you love Me and seek to know Me better. But you cannot know Me in a vacuum, Debbie. You meet Me in the people and situations I place in your path. And right now, Debbie, that is Peg. I want you to respect and obey her while I teach you about respect and obedience."

I felt as horror-struck as Debbie looked. Respect? Obedience? Had those words actually come from my mouth?

Abruptly Debbie got up and raced from the stable. "Well that's that," I said to myself. "She's gone to pack and head for home."

But when, a quarter of an hour later, I followed her down to the house, I walked in on an amazing scene. Debbie was folded in Peg's arms, sobbing her heart out on Peg's shoulder, and Peg was murmuring the soothing phrases any mother uses to a hurt and tired child . . .

It was the beginning of a new relationship, one in which Debbie tried—more and more successfully—to let her headstrong, impulsive nature be guided by Peg's wiser, more disciplined one. The amazing thing to me was that it seemed to work. Debbie, the freest, brightest spirit I'd ever known, lost none of her sparkle, none of her vitality, but gained something of Peg's deep-running peace. It stunned and fascinated me.

For reasons I did not understand, it also scared me to death.

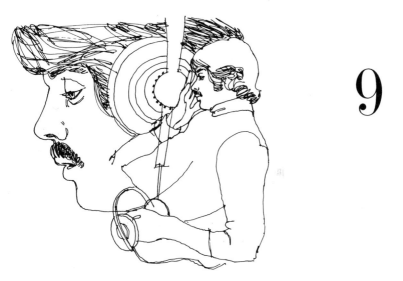

Another winter was coming—and what would happen then to all the things that were going on at the barn? The musical weekends, bigger than ever now that colleges were back in full swing. The daily crowd of kids who came out to work and to find Jesus. The six or seven people who were living now at Love Inn. Already on crisp fall days you could see your breath inside the place.

I asked around to find out what it would cost to put some kind of insulation on the walls, and even the cheapest was out of the question. Then one day Peg called me at our apartment to say that a friend of hers who ran a sawmill had made us an offer of some slab wood.

"What's slab wood?" I asked.

"When you saw up a log for lumber," Peg explained patiently, "the outside layers with the bark on them are called slab wood. The man said they don't have much value except as fuel."

"Well, we don't have our fireplace built yet, but I guess . . ."

"He did say people sometimes use it as building material."

Building material! Suddenly I could see it. If we used the barky slab wood as siding, nailing it around the outside of the barn, we would have an excellent insulation against the cold and also create a kind of log cabin effect. I told Peg we'd accept as much of the wood as we could get, and within a few days our hammers and saws were singing as we began the long process of giving our barn a second wall.

Building the fireplace was urgent now too. We got hold of some second-hand bricks and started laying it at the spot where I'd seen it in my vision. Only we couldn't seem to make much progress. Once it pulled away from the wall, once it fell down altogether. We were putting it up a third time when the laconic old codger who'd helped us about the center post in the loft paid us a visit. He looked at the hayloft theater and nodded his head in silent approval. When I took him on a tour of the rest of the barn he had only one thing to say. As we passed the brick fireplace he mumbled:

"Won't draw."

Next day we tore the whole thing down and stacked the brick outside. And now a recurrent theme began cropping up in my daily Bible reading. Building materials. Every passage I read, the Israelites were constructing something or other. And brick, every time, was the symbol of slavery. Stone, now, that was something else! Throughout the Bible, rock and stone was the symbol for Jesus. The light, the warmth, the fellowship, all the good things we hoped to enjoy around our fireplace, should be founded on stone.

So throughout the fall, while the trees on the hills turned orange and scarlet, we roamed the fields around the farm gathering stone left behind by the glaciers that had formed the landscape itself. Now the actual construction went rapidly. Before long we were burning scraps from our work to keep us warm. The fireplace roared its approval.

I saw something else as I stood admiring the massive grey stone mantel and chimney. Brick is made by man, stone by God. As with the thick slab wood which shielded us from wind and cold more efficiently than any artificial insulation could have done, God seemed to be saying,

I alone am building this place and I will provide everything you need.

He did it in the most startling ways. Like the time Peg pointed out how much money we could save on food if we had a freezer to take advantage of specials and seasonal prices.

"I don't mean just a little one, Scott. We need a big commercial freezer."

We were feeding dozens of people at the barn almost every day now. Scores, on our musical weekends. Peg, Ken, Debbie, Nedra and I, and six or seven other Love Inn regulars were sitting around our storeroom-library for what we'd come to call a "family meeting."

"Let's pray about it," someone said.

So I plunged in. "Lord, You hear Peg's request. We need a freezer. A large one. A commercial freezer so we can put up meat and vegetables and things in season." The telephone rang. "So I ask You, please, Lord . . ." The telephone continued to ring, ". . . to answer our request . . ." The telephone would not stop ringing. Impatiently I snatched up the receiver.

"Love Inn. Scott Ross speaking."

And then I almost dropped the phone.

"I'm sorry to bother you," a lady was saying, "but my husband and I are closing the frozen food section in our store and we wonder if by any chance you people could use a large commercial freezer?"

Or the time we needed some cement. The make-shift little kitchen we'd been getting along on wasn't anything like big enough for the weekend turnouts. We needed the kitchen I'd seen in that glimpse of the finished barn—and that meant laying a concrete foundation. Well, we prayed for the cement to make it with, as we'd prayed for every need since the freezer experience, and began to work on the excavation.

A week later the foundation was dug and the forms in place. Still no cement. Around mid-morning the work was interrupted by a visitor. It was a lady who lived about a mile away and would occasionally bring us eggs or tomatoes, but who made no bones about being leery of all this prayer business. I wasn't there that day but I heard later how she approached the two young college men who were working on the forms.

"I'm just looking around," she said. She always started like that. "What's all this going to be?" She waved her hand at the excavation.

They told her. They also told her a bit shyly how we were counting on God to supply the cement.

"Don't you think that's being naive?" the woman said.

They didn't have a chance to answer. A sharp hissing sound from the highway made them look up. There, looming over them on the rise into Peg's drive was . . . a huge cement truck.

The driver climbed out. He lumbered down the driveway and stood in front of the young men chomping on a cigar.

"Could you use some cement?" he asked.

They looked at the woman and shrugged. "Lady," one of them said, "if you want to know the truth I'm not sure I believe this either."

The woman began to query the driver. Did he know the people at Love Inn? No. Did he know they were putting in a new kitchen? No. Was he giving away the cement? Yes, it was left over from a job and he'd been going to dump it. He didn't know why he had stopped here; as he was driving by he just had a hunch to pull over. "But look," he said, shifting his cigar from one side of his mouth to the other, "either you want it or you don't."

"Oh, we want it!" the young men said. And within minutes the truck had backed up to the forms, and was filling them with the fresh cement. As for the lady, they told me she got into her car and patched out as she took off down Route 13.

These things filled us with awe and joy, although oddly enough they seemed to disturb a lot of the radio audience when I told about them on the air. "When you snap your finger God comes running, doesn't He?" one man wrote.

Maybe he had a point? Were we really being thankful enough—humbled enough—by these homey miracles? Remembering Nedra's and my decision back in Hagerstown never to ask for something new until we had thanked God for what He had already done, I put up a bulletin board on the wall of the barn. We divided it into two columns. At the top of the first were the words *Be thank-ful for all things*. And beneath it were listed the things we had most recently to be grateful for:

* cement
* rug remnants
* paint for the bathroom

The other column was headed *Ask and it shall be given you*. Beneath this we put down items we were currently praying for:

* glue that will really stick for wallpaper
* a decent hammer
* a door knob for the toilet
* one red and white Volkswagen bus in excellent condition

"The exact make and model of the car you want?" a student from Rensselaer Polytechnic asked on a visit to the barn. "Even complete with the color! Doesn't that sound a little like dictating to God?"

I thought back to the family meeting when that particular request had gone up on the board. It was obvious we needed wheels out at the barn. Nedra and I had the Karman Ghia, but that wasn't big enough to haul things in, and anyhow it wasn't there most of the time. When someone needed to get into town he generally had to hitchhike. "How about a second-hand Volkswagen bus?" somebody said. "They're pretty cheap to run."

"As long as it's not so old it has to be in the repair shop all the time," another added.

"I saw a red and white one in town yesterday," I threw in. "Gee, it was beautiful!"

And so we'd written not just our need, but our dream, up on our prayer list. Was this attempting to give God orders, like the Rensselaer guy said?

And then I remembered something.

"You know," I told him, "when I was a little kid back in Glas-gow, I used to dream of owning black, patent leather sandals.

My father didn't have a lot of money, but the next time I needed shoes he bought those sandals. I loved them more than any shoes I ever had. But what I chiefly remember is Dad—the pleasure it gave him to be able to provide not just what I needed, but my heart's desire."

The guy looked unconvinced. "Well, if God offers you a green and black Ford pick-up, I wouldn't throw it back in His face."

But while we waited for the outcome of this one, God continued to meet our physical needs in crazy abundance. I'll never forget one Saturday noon when there must have been over a hundred people standing in line for lunch. Nedra, Peg and Debbie had fixed two huge pots of stew, but it was obvious there wasn't going to be enough. The line of kids stretched from the kitchen pass-through out the door of the barn and clear around the side.

The first pot was scraped clean, the second one was getting low. Nedra, ladling out the food at the pass-through window, could see the bottom fast approaching, and still the hungry people kept coming.

And at that point a station wagon pulled into Peg's driveway and out stepped two middle-aged ladies, each one carrying a large flat pan. They came through the side door into the kitchen.

"I hope you don't mind," one of them said, "but last night while we were praying we had the strongest feeling that we ought to make a lot of lasagna and bring it over to Love Inn. So here it is."

Nedra put the last helping of stew on the plate before her. Her heart missed a beat, but her ladle never did, as she dug into the steaming trays of food.

And if His material provision was a source of wonder, His action in people's hearts and minds was even more so. Scarcely a day passed now without some story of changed lives. Like Todd and Miriam who roared into Ithaca on a Honda 750 enroute to nowhere. They'd started out in Florida and covered a lot of territory, very sure of what they were leaving behind, less sure of where they were going and what they'd find if they got there.

They came out of a diner in Ithaca to discover that both their helmets had been stolen from their bike. By the time they'd located a motorcycle shop and bought new ones, it was late. The guy in the motorcycle place thought there was a barn up the road where people sometimes spent the night.

And so Todd and Miriam arrived at Love Inn. And the overnight stop-off turned into a twelve-month stay as both of them found the direction they had been seeking in their lives.

It was happening around us all the time. And so . . . why did I continue to see so little change in myself? Oh, on the surface I was a real redeemed character, Mr. Helpful himself. But inside, where only I and a few bruised friends and relations knew about them, were the same quick temper, the same paranoia, the same secret thought life I'd been plagued with so long.

I was beginning to see that there was a common denominator to all of these battle areas. My ego. I remember the tragic car accident that let me see how deep rooted the problem was.

Late one afternoon after I'd gone up to the station, a car and a truck collided on Route 13 near Kirk Road. The driver of the car was killed and the passenger, a teenaged girl, was rushed to the hospital in critical condition. Since it happened not far from the barn, several people from Love Inn helped out at the scene; afterward one of them called to tell me about it and ask me to pray for the girl.

I did, both then with the staff at CBN, and later that evening over the air. In fact I made quite a personal crusade of it, getting a radio prayer-campaign started, driving to the hospital myself after the show to visit her. She was in a coma, scarcely alive to all appearances, but as I prayed and read the Bible in the corridor outside her room, I had that experience of words seeming to stand out from the page. It was in the last chapter of Mark, where the three women come to Jesus' tomb. *He is risen,* an angel tells them; *he is not here.*

It was a message straight to me from God! The girl too would rise from that hospital bed! All the next day I proclaimed her total healing, in spite of all medical signs to the contrary. Over the radio that night I announced that we were about to witness a miracle like those recorded in the Bible. "I have the scripture for it," I told the audience, "and God cannot go back on His word."

During the next record Andy Andersen came into the studio. "Didn't you hear, Scott? That young girl died half an hour ago."

Well, I went into a kind of prolonged spiritual pout. For weeks I refused to pray for healing at all. God had led me along and then He'd let me down.

One afternoon I was in Syracuse doing a remote broadcast for CBN at the New York State Fair. From a portable studio in a trailer truck I would wander through the crowd with a microphone on a long extension cord, doing on-the-spot interviews.

All at once I noticed a lady being pushed through the throng in a wheelchair. And at that moment into my mind sprang a scene, complete with dialogue and everything. In that scenario I approached the crippled lady with my microphone and asked her if she would like Jesus to heal her.

"Oh yes!"

I saw myself lay my hand on her head: "In the name of Jesus, stand up and walk!" I imagined her leaping from her chair, walking, skipping, dancing, while a wondering crowd gathered about us (and an awestruck radio audience listened at home). And then I saw the lady point to me and heard her say,

"He did it!"

He did it! The crowd took up the cry. Scott Ross did it! Scott Ross healed her!

The imaginary scene faded, but not the horror that had seized me as I got a look at myself. I dashed back to the broadcast truck and climbed into the back, shaking with that knowledge. When that young girl had died in Ithaca, what had upset me most—the tragedy? Or the fact that I'd looked foolish?

He is risen; he is not here. Perhaps I thought suddenly, God *had* been speaking to me in that verse. The girl had not been there, on that bed in the hospital room: the real person had risen and was in bliss with Jesus. But I hadn't been listening for God's word on the situation. Scott Ross had prayed for physical healing, and Scott Ross couldn't hear anything else.

How could God use me for healing if I did not listen? How could He use me for anything, I wondered wretchedly as the electronic gadgetry around me clicked and hummed, if my own ego got involved in every situation? If I appropriated the wisdom and glory that belonged to Him?

Now that I'd identified the problem, I saw how ego was mixed up in everything. Recently I'd turned an old grain storage area at the barn into an office where I could answer mail from the radio show. Now I noticed how much coming and going there was around Love Inn. True to the original vision, the barn was never closed. People came and went at all hours of the day and night. Strangers walked in off the highway. But I had private correspondence, a record collection, books, in that office. No, I'd put in a door and have a solid lock put on it. I announced my decision at the family meeting next morning.

General indignation. This was an infraction of freedom! Everything at the barn should be available to everyone! It showed lack of trust in the Lord!

I felt the familiar anger rising inside me. "I've made my mind up," I snapped, "and that's the way it's going to be."

The book room emptied in a hurry, leaving behind an atmosphere of discord and antagonism. I got down on my knees on the many-colored rug as I had had to do so often lately. "Lord, there goes my mouth again. Won't I ever change? Won't I ever be any different?"

I prayed for an hour asking Him to show me who was right in this situation. But: "In My sight," I seemed to hear Him say, "it isn't a question of who's right and who's wrong." *All of you be subject one to another.* Those words that I'd kept trying to dodge around in the first letter of Peter wouldn't go out of my head. Christians, God seemed to be telling me, were to yield to each other in love, not be out winning battles.

I got up off my knees, rounded up everyone I could locate, and called another meeting in the book room. My face burning, I asked forgiveness for my high-handed approach. "This should be a group decision, not any one person's. Whatever we decide together, that's what we'll do."

And with those words a remarkable change took place. If rebellion was contagious, so was yieldedness. Suddenly the steam went out of the situation. Instead of pressing this point of view or that, we started seeking God's viewpoint. I said hardly a word as the others, one by one, brought up the values of privacy, the need to protect property. The decision of the meeting was to install the door and the lock. But if I felt a sense of triumph it had nothing to do with that; it was that we'd tasted the sweetness of a right relationship.

Learning to think as "we" instead of "I"—here and there, now and then, I was beginning to do it. But there was one subject I knew I could never lay before the group. How could I share with anyone else the struggles I was having with my thought life? In the days before I became a Christian my sex life was pretty free-wheeling. When Nedra and I walked to the front of the church in Hagerstown, I knew that, among other things, the actual sex adventuring had to stop, and it did. Only, there was an interior sex life—a fantasy life—that kept right on. It was, I said to myself, an innocent enough way to handle drives that the Lord had given me and I made no special attempt to stop it.

When Nedra and I were married I expected that the thoughts would go away. But they didn't. They were just another expression of me going my own way. And in the end this cost me a great deal at Love Inn.

The problem was this. The most frequent problem area for the young people who came to the barn was sex. From masturbation and sex before marriage, to homosexuality and a lot weirder perversions, they were generally hung up on sex in one way or another. When people talked with me about their problems they didn't want theories, they wanted help that worked. If I hadn't won the battle myself, what could I tell them? Whenever I talked to some guy about the beauty of sex the way God created it to be, I could see in his eyes that I wasn't getting through.

So the old unyielded self was creating difficulties. And the biggest one of all was at CBN.

Andy Andersen and I were at loggerheads. Andy felt we should be serving the local Christian community, the farmers and businessmen where the station's support came from. I wanted to reach the uncommitted college audience. His listeners complained about my programming, and vice versa.

The two groups not only disagreed about music and style of speech but often about the content of what was said too. On *Tell It Like It Is* we talked about the Baptism in the Holy Spirit, about the gifts of the Spirit, about healing, guidance, miracles. One day I prayed for a sick pony a little girl wrote in about. The phone was ringing before the amen. Healing was okay for the Bible but not for now. Most especially, one should never pray for animals.

And then came the issue of the fund drive. Andy pointed out—and the ledger backed him up—that unless more money came in, the station would have to shut down. Someone had an idea. We would ask people to make donations of physical items: a television set, books, clothes. Then we would auction these off for cash over the air.

I didn't like the idea. I made myself a nuisance around the mountain transmitter, complaining to every ear. This was huckstering; we were depending on man's cleverness instead of God's supply. At last one night I voiced my criticism on the air.

"I'm sorry good people," I said into the mike, sitting in the studio high in the hills. "I just can't keep silent. This fund raising approach is wrong. We need money, sure, but we shouldn't raise it by barter. If this is the Lord's project, He will find the money . . ." On and on I went.

The next night Andy called me into his office and talked to me about anarchy, how impossible it was to run a radio station without a chain of command. If I didn't feel I could live with his decisions, perhaps I didn't belong at CBN-Northeast.

"I don't belong anywhere," I answered grandly, "where man's

ways are put ahead of God's." And with that I quit, little aware
that the Lord was going to use this experience to teach me a lesson
I didn't want to learn.

I drove home bursting to explode to Nedra about all the things
the station was doing wrong. But she met me at the door of the
apartment with an anxious frown:

"Scott, it's two o'clock and Nedra Kristina still hasn't gotten to
sleep. Every time she lies down that awful wheezing and gasping
begins." We went upstairs and sat down on the side of Nedra
Kristina's bed. She was wide awake, hair matted with perspiration,
dark circles of exhaustion under her large brown eyes.

I lifted our two-year-old onto my lap. "Lord Jesus," I said, "we
know this sickness isn't Your will." I remembered the prayer I had
made in the hospital after she was born. "In Your name, Jesus,
I take authority over whatever force of evil it is that is attacking
our little girl."

Later, in our own bedroom, I got to worrying about that. Here
I was trying to take authority when I wouldn't submit to authority.
Had I been wrong to walk out on Andy? As I tossed on my bed
I seemed to hear the answer: "Your rebellion is blocking your
prayers for your child. Remember that all authority is ordained
by Me; when you rebel against it you are rebelling against Me.
When you learn this lesson, Nedra Kristina will be healed."

Could I possibly be hearing right? I had always skipped over
such ideas in the Bible. They had too much the ring of a feudal
lord's propaganda for keeping his serfs in line. "Your station in
life is ordained by God, you miserable slave, so you just stay in
your place."

But all night long, as the background to my thoughts, came the
sound of our little girl's labored breathing.

I redoubled my efforts now to line up speaking dates; this would
be our only source of income until I found another job. Then, one
morning in the mail, I found an invoice for some books I had
ordered. They'd been delivered to the station up on the hill. I'd
have to drive up there and get them.

As I drove along, past our old trailer home, past fields of rocky pastureland, that familiar voice inside my head was back again.

"Why are you going up to CBN?"

"Why am I going? To pick up a carton of books."

"No," came the voice, "that's not the reason. You are going up there to tell Andy Andersen you were wrong. You are going back to apologize, and to submit yourself to him."

I pulled over to the side of the road and shut off the motor. The countryside was immensely quiet. "But Lord, I'm not wrong. *He's* wrong. I want to be in submission to You, not to men," I said.

"You were never in submission to men."

"Wasn't I?"

"No! Look how You overthrew the money changers in the Temple."

"The money changers weren't in authority over Me."

"Well, then . . . all those religious laws, about healing on the Sabbath and everything."

"Being in submission doesn't mean being silent about error. Submitted men are not yes-men."

"What does it mean then, being in submission?"

"It means recognizing your place in an order. You to authority, authority to God. Workers to employers. Children to parents. Wives to husbands, husbands to Christ, Christ to the Father. But at every point in every chain each person must speak the truth as he sees it. Your job is to speak the truth, authority's job is to decide what to do about it. They decided to put Me on a cross. Am I asking you to do anything as costly as that?"

I sat there for a long time, while a woodchuck appeared in the field and slowly nibbled his way to within a yard of the car. At last I switcned on the motor, dreading what lay ahead. I took the rest of the hill in low gear, not even raising a cloud of dust.

To my huge relief, Andy was not at the station. Five other staffers were, though. "Hello, Scott. We never expected to see you back here."

We stood around in the kitchen of the old farmhouse. Someone handed me a cup of coffee; it rattled in its saucer.

"I've come back to tell you all I'm sorry," I said, swallowing back tears. "The Lord has been showing me . . ."

And just at that moment Andy's car pulled up to the back door. He walked into the kitchen and stiffened as he saw me. I suppose he thought I'd come back to campaign again for my ideas.

I walked over to him and for a moment we stood face to face. I could hear the news teletype ticking away in the next room.

"Andy," I said. I could not hold his eyes. "Andy, I was wrong. You're the manager of this station and I tried to usurp your role. I'm sorry."

Well it was a pretty emotional scene. I was weeping after all. Andy put his hand on my shoulder and told me I could start back to work anytime.

So I did. But wow. Going up there to submit had been hard, and it kept on being hard. I think maybe in some part of me I'd expected that after I submitted, Andy would come around to my side—like at the barn when I submitted the question of the office door and got my own way. Not this time. Andy and I simply had two different approaches. We were trying to reach two separate audiences. Andy came straight to the point.

"Scott, don't play any more rock music."

I started to explode, then checked myself. "All right, Andy." I had spoken the truth as I saw it, now I submitted to the man in authority over me "as unto the Lord," as the Bible says. I didn't like the musical results, but I tried desperately not to show it. "You're going to obey Andy," I said to myself, "and you're going to be cheerful about it."

So for a month I sat up at the station spinning tweedle-dum and tweedle-dee music and avoiding controversial topics on the air. Almost at once I noticed changes, not so much at work as in other areas. As I began to get into the right relationship with Andy, I discovered that Nedra and I were bickering less. We'd been hearing all the talk about how the wife was supposed to submit to her husband. Now we saw that it was the husband, not the wife, who was the primary "submitted" one in the family. He was to be submitted to the Lord. The wife's role was to trust that attitude.

There were other encouragements. One night while I was on the air a telephone call came through.

"My name is Peggy Nichols. I live in Brockport, New York. My husband's in the auto body business."

"Oh?"

Then she started telling me about a badly smashed-up Volkswagen bus which had come into the shop. I held my breath. "The owner has decided not to keep it, but my husband thinks it can be fixed up almost like new. There's nothing wrong with the engine."

When it was ready, she said, they were going to donate it to Love Inn. And so a couple of weeks later Nedra and I drove to Brockport.

The Nichols were as excited as children. Mr. Nichols threw open the door to his garage shop and Nedra and I burst out laughing and crying all at once. For the bus was, of course, painted a bright shiny red, with white trim.

That afternoon back at the barn we checked off "one red and white VW bus in excellent condition" from our Prayer and Praise board.

But the most wonderful answer of all came so quietly we scarcely noticed it. Local doctors continued to be baffled by Nedra Kristina's stubborn bronchitis. At last they recommended a consultation with a specialist in Syracuse. And so, with considerable difficulty, an appointment was set up.

We never kept it.

On the day before we were scheduled to go, Nedra said to me: "Guess what, honey?"

"I give up what."

"We've been so busy trying to set up this date we haven't been using our eyes and ears. Nedra's been breathing fine lately! She hasn't had a sleepless night in . . . in . . ."

"A month?"

It was one month since I had submitted my opinion about the radio show to Andy Andersen.

"A month," said Nedra. "She hasn't had a sleepless night in a month."

It was Thanksgiving weekend, 1969. I had just come back from a speaking date and was crawling into bed at one o'clock in the morning when downstairs in the den the telephone rang. I ran down and picked up the receiver.

"Praise God, brother!" It was the husky, unmistakable voice of Harald Bredesen. "I'm at Pat Robertson's," he went on.

Then Pat's voice was on another extension. It seemed that as he and Harald had been praying that evening, God had begun speaking to them about a brand new type of radio show. And suddenly I found myself telling the two of them about the dream God had dropped full-blown into my head down in Roanoke.

"The key," I said, "is that the program wouldn't go out over Christian outlets. It would be a give-away show aimed at commercial radio stations across the country."

Before we hung up that night we were talking about a three-hour prime-time format geared to general radio. In December Nedra and I went to Pat's and Dede's home in Portsmouth and actually began putting things together. The name of the program, Pat said, would be the Scott Ross Show.

"Oh no. Pat, I've been fighting this ego thing for months now." I described a few recent failures in this area.

"But it's got to be that way," Pat said. "People relate to a person, not a title. And we can let you have Larry." Larry Black was a top notch production and marketing man from CBN-Northeast. It was a real index of Pat's excitement that he would let us have Larry.

And so I left my job at the Ithaca station. Left it not in rebellion and anger, but in God's timing, and for His purpose—with the best wishes of Andy Andersen ringing in my ears.

Within weeks we were making our pilot program, using CBN facilities in Ithaca. Before long 16 stations were using the show and we were getting a hundred letters a week from listeners. It was hopeless trying to answer them all. I was at my typewriter late at night and early in the morning: the questions people were asking and the problems they were facing would tear you apart. About this time I was in New York City to give a talk about Love Inn when a young black girl introduced herself. "I don't suppose you need a secretary up there," she said. A few weeks later Jacki Brown joined the staff of the Scott Ross Show.

We were acquiring other full-timers. One day in the spring of 1970, into my office came Jim Harrington, a shy, lanky, slow-talking college student who for months had been spending week-ends at the barn.

"Hi, Scott."

It was rare to hear Jim put even two words together. I said "Hi" back and waited.

"I graduated."

I thought hastily. Then I remembered: Jim had been studying agriculture at the State University of New York at Cobbleskill. "Congratulations. What are you going to do now?"

"I was wondering," said Jim, "if you could use somebody to manage this farm. You know, grow some real crops. Breed live-stock."

Jim was one of the first residents in the new dorm rooms Ken Spafard was helping us build where the pony stalls had been. Jim taught us organic gardening and started upgrading our small stock of cows, sheep, pigs and rabbits. One evening a few weeks after Jim moved in, I saw Debbie coming out of Peg's house wearing a dress . . . I hadn't known she owned such a thing.

"Going out with Jim again, Debbie?" Each weekend the funniest sight at the barn had been silent, down-to-earth Jim trailing about after the whirlwind which was Debbie.

But that night as I watched Jim holding the door of the red and white VW, and saw Deb demurely gather her skirt as she climbed in, I suddenly knew that Love Inn was going to produce its first marriage.

What a celebration it was, on July 11, 1970—all of us gathered on the lawn next to Peg's house as Debbie and Jim became Mr. and Mrs. Harrington.

How much the Lord had done, I thought, in the year and a half since Nedra and I first drove out Route 13 to see a tumble-down barn. I looked at the handsome bark-sided building, the parking lot jammed with cars, the joyful faces all around us.

And yet, in a way, the very success of the place was proving a boomerang.

We should have seen it coming. More and more people swarmed over us. No one knew Johnny from Charlie or Annie from Margaret. Each person did his own thing; in fact one guy wrote a ditty that became a kind of theme song for a while:

L-O-V-E I-N-N
You can do your thing at
Love Inn!

It was chaos. No one was working. No one took directions. Many Sunday mornings after an evening of music I'd come out to the barn to find 30 bodies sprawled all over the place.

Around noon they'd start to wander into the kitchen: "Hey, what's to eat?"

We tried to solve the problem by leaving the kitchen to the visitors themselves. But that didn't work either. They wasted food, left bread out, never put the lid on the peanut butter jar, never washed up. If they wanted to put something in the trash, they made a basketball shot at it.

With the lack of organization and the thin pickings for money, we considered several times just closing our doors. One day in early September 1970, I finished recording the Scott Ross Show and went out to the barn around 2:00 P.M. I opened the door and literally stumbled across the body of a teenager wrapped in a serape, asleep on the floor. The boy woke up angry. "What's the idea, man? I'm trying to sleep!" He rolled over with his back to me.

Well, I mulled that over all day. Not that there was anything unusual about the scene. That was the trouble. I felt like heaving the kid out, and yet—was there anything really wrong, morally, spiritually wrong, with sleeping at two in the afternoon? Whenever I was tempted to make rules for the barn: everybody up at such and such an hour, meals at such and such a time, I'd remember the rule-dominated religion of my childhood where there were so many restrictions and regulations that the joy and excitement of Christ got lost.

But that same evening I suddenly knew I had had enough. Nedra and I had finished supper and put little Nedra down hours ago. I was trying to work on a talk, but I kept staring off into nothing.

"What's the matter, honey?" Nedra asked. I told her about the guy in the serape.

"Do you know what I'm going to do?" I said. "I'm going out to the barn right now and I'm going to stay there until I hear from God about this whole mess."

"I'll be praying too, Scott," said Nedra.

So I drove out to Love Inn. It was after midnight, and only a few people were still talking around the remains of a fire. I went upstairs to my office, especially glad now that there was a door to close. I got out Dad's chain-reference Bible and began to delve into the whole subject of order and discipline on the one hand, freedom on the other. The more I followed the various headings, the more I saw that even Jesus Himself had not been free to come and go as He chose; He was constantly under the authority of His Father. Nor were His followers free: Jesus was not only their Saviour but their Master. Always, it seemed, there was a chain of command. But not at Love Inn.

"Why are you ducking authority, son?" that inner voice asked.

"First you didn't want to be under authority, now you don't want to exercise authority."

"That can't be You, Lord? You know how I've longed for freedom. I don't want to be a wet nurse to a lot of alienated kids."

The voice was silent.

"And besides, I've had no experience in leading." That was true enough. "And I have too many weaknesses in my own life to start telling others how to live."

"Now we're getting to the heart of it, aren't we? You're afraid of hypocrisy."

Little did I dream of the dramas which would grow out of that thought. At the time though, I slid right over it. "What's wrong with each person getting his directions straight from You?"

"Nothing at all."

I felt relief. So I was off the hook!

"But you still don't act in isolation. You get what you believe are My orders, then you check them out with the church. Always and forever, Scott, the key to life in the Spirit is not independence. It is membership in My Body on earth."

The voice was silent a while, then went on.

"It's true I didn't come to lay a lot of rules on people, but I did set forth principles. See what you can do to bring some pattern to your life together."

Which is how *Patterns* came into being. That same night sitting in my office at Love Inn, I jotted down a set of principles that might help us bring a semblance of order out of our confusion. Surely it was a Biblical principle, I wrote down, to seek the Lord early? And shouldn't we seek Him together? Shouldn't we bring structure to our dealing with strangers, by being sure each visitor was met and talked to? Shouldn't we interview newcomers to find out what their needs were—even just what their names were? Why should one guy hang around for a couple of days, another for a couple of months? Maybe we could develop a Five Day Program to spell out what Love Inn meant. And work—certainly work had a sound scriptural basis.

I read over my notes, discovering how tentative and apologetic they sounded. I went over the pages again and this time stated the principles more crisply. Schedule. Discipline. Work. Order. These were the words that kept coming up as I struggled on through the night.

I was appalled at myself. I couldn't believe that I—Mr. Rebellion himself—was really writing this.

Next day at the barn I showed the draft of *Patterns* to the first guy I met. He read it and whistled.

"This is going to make waves."

"Any changes?"

"Yes. You're not being Biblical about the wine." I had written "no wine" at Love Inn, but he was right. Besides that would be a rule, not a principle. So I struck it out and stated instead that excess in anything was not honoring God's intent for our lives. A little later that day, I called a meeting in the book room.

Knowing from my own struggles how nerve-touching the whole subject of discipline and order was, I opened with a long, heartfelt prayer. Then I read *Patterns* aloud.

There was a numbed silence, then an explosion of protests. All the objections I myself had raised were voiced aloud:

"What are you trying to do, set yourself up as some kind of spiritual know-it-all?"

"You'll drive everyone away from the place."

"I'll seek the Lord when I feel like it, and that may not be in the morning."

"No one's going to tell me what job to do when I'm working for free!"

When a little of the hysteria had died down, a wise and loving black woman spoke up. "Scott," Lucille said softly, "you are quenching the Spirit."

I felt all of the conviction drain out of me. This, of course, was the great danger. I had no answer. The room fell silent, but it was one of those silences that is really an uproar.

So we broke up. Nothing more was said about *Patterns* for the time being, but already that night there were fewer people at the barn for supper. I felt a great heaviness as I started for home.

Within a week, 20 people who had been camping out in the barn had moved on. Some were simply freeloaders and I wasn't sorry to see them go. Others however struck me as the very alternate-society types we had been trying to reach. I saw their forlorn silhouettes walking slowly down the highway, bedrolls on their backs.

Patterns scared away some newcomers too. Others that did stay were of a slightly different type, a little older, a little more serious about wanting to see change in their lives. In the end there was a shaking down at Love Inn. I had intended to hold a second meeting where we would discuss the different items in *Patterns,* and then either accept or reject it, but it proved unnecessary. By the end of one week there were only a dozen "permanents" left at Love Inn, and we all agreed that Jesus' own example was far from the go-your-own-way mood that had been ours up until now.

Patterns had become part of Love Inn.

One day shortly after this trauma, I was walking over to the barn with Peg when I saw a striking figure wandering around the grounds, following Jim Harrington. The guy was all beard. When he got closer I could see dark deep-set eyes, piercing and strong.

"Who's the guy with the big black beard?" I asked Peg.

"His name is Joe Laiacona," Peg said.

"Joseph of Egypt would be more like it."

When I had a chance I introduced myself to this patriarch. Joe told me he came from Albany. He was a Roman Catholic who until recently had been studying for the priesthood. He read *Patterns* and shook his head. It reminded him, he said, of the strict rules at his seminary—rules he'd worried even there about being able to keep.

I was surprised, then, when Joe asked if he could stick around. Joe Laiacona was one of the very first people to go through the new Five Day Program of introduction to Love Inn.

At the end of that time he announced that he wanted to stay. "Furthermore," he said, "I'll volunteer to take over the kitchen. I was assistant chef at a summer camp once and I enjoyed it."

Here was welcome news indeed. The kitchen continued to be a disaster area. Not during the week so much, any more, but the weekends continued to attract large crowds. "You can't cook for 150 people using these family-sized pots," said Joe, tossing our kitchenware into a cardboard box. "And you can't buy on a nickel and dime basis. You have to plan ahead. Buy in bulk."

"Where's the money to come from, Joe?" asked bookkeeper Peg.

"Prayer."

In the dubious silence, he went on to tell us that he had just ordered $500 worth of food to be delivered the following Wednesday.

"Well, God will *have* to provide," said Peg checking the account book. "We've got $80 to our name."

"Good," Joe said. "Write me a check for that much. That'll be our down payment. We'll pray for the rest to be here by Wednesday."

But that weekend Joe took off to visit his girlfriend, Ann Costello. "Now don't let me down," he said cheerily. "I want to see the larder full when I get back. And I want to see the whole shipment paid for."

We did pray, hard. Wednesday came. At noon the truck arrived from the wholesaler.

"Where do you want me to put this stuff?" the driver asked, jerking his head at the restaurant-sized cans of ketchup and mustard, the hundred-pound sacks of sugar and flour, the cases of frozen food. We showed him the kitchen, rounded up a few strong backs to help him unload, then checked with Peg. Had any money come in the mail? None. Was there any in the Love Buckets in the barn? Only $20. Great. We were $400 short and by now most of the food was stashed away in the freezer and kitchen shelves.

A car drove into the driveway. Out stepped Mia Hansen, the very first person to be converted as a result of the *Tell It Like It Is* radio show more than a year earlier. Mia was married now and didn't get out to the barn much. But in her hand was a check.

"This just came from my mother," she said. "I want Love Inn to have it."

The check was for $400.

When we told Joe about the way the Lord had met the grocery bill he was pleased but not especially surprised. "It's the Lord's way of saying we're on the right track," he said. "Now, for Thanksgiving weekend we'd better plan on a crowd Friday as well as Saturday . . ."

Joe was clearly a natural leader, but he was far from being a natural cook. Heavy starches, greases, fats—it must have been a concentration camp where he was assistant chef. "Well, Joe," said Nedra, pushing aside mounds of nearly raw dough to reveal a tea-spoonful of apple in Joe's apple tart, "now we know why you weren't promoted to chef."

"Never mind," said Joe. "My cooking is good for your faith. Haven't you read," he added, pouring out a cup of tar-colored coffee, "that if ye drink any deadly thing it will not hurt you?"

In the end the Lord moved Joe out of the kitchen. He was constantly being called away to counsel with a new arrival, or to discuss with Peg how much new paint we could afford to order. Bit by bit the food responsibility fell back on the shoulders of the women at Love Inn. We've been praising the Lord ever since for our deliverance.

By the end of Joe's first year at the barn, things had settled into a routine. Every week I'd go to the CBN studio to record the three-hour Scott Ross Show. The show was now on 40 stations and Jacki had to have help answering the mail. Peg gave us another piece of land to go with the barn. After the original shakedown, *Patterns* hadn't affected the numbers of people wanting to become part of Love Inn; it just attracted a great group: Paul Freed, Bill Clarke, Glorya Garafola, Ted Sandquist.

Ted was a twenty-three-year-old who first read about us in an article in the *New York Times*. He came up and moved into the dorm room next to Joe's. The two of them made a fantastic team: Joe's black bush beside Ted's trim, honey-colored hair, Joe's burning black eyes and Ted's mild blue ones.

Christian Scott Ross was born in November 1971. We got an insight into how our neighbors were starting to accept us when the time came to pay the hospital bill. One of the principles in *Patterns* was service to the community. Love-Inners had been doing volunteer work all over town, among other places at the hospital. When I went into the cashier's office the day Nedra and Christian Scott were ready to come home, the lady behind the desk opened her own pocketbook. "That's a great place you've got out there," she said, and handed me twenty dollars toward the bill.

139

In other words, things were going great.

So great that for long periods of time I could actually kid my-self that the old, unreconstructed Scott was dead and buried. Then something would happen to show that he was still alive and kick-ing. Like the visit from the local fire marshal. He inspected the living quarters we had built in the old pony stalls.

"How many people are living here on a regular basis?" he asked as he peered into the last of the little rooms.

I was wary. "Quite a few," I said. No, that wasn't good enough. "Seventeen."

The marshal asked more questions, made more notes. Then came the verdict. We were violating every safety regulation in the book. Unless the violations were corrected in 30 days we would have to close the dormitory.

Well I hit the ceiling. Who were the nit-picking legalists who had nothing better to do than think up stupid regulations. Ted Sandquist and Joe Laiacona halted my tirade:

"Christians are told to obey the laws of the state, Scott. First Peter 3:13 makes it about as clear as it can be: 'Submit yourselves to every ordinance of man for the Lord's sake.'"

There I was once again. In rebellion against authority.

"And if I'm a German," I said, "and the Nazis tell me to put some little Jewish kid in the oven?"

"Then it's a moral issue and you have a higher law to follow. But there's nothing immoral about putting in a fire alarm." And without another glance in my direction Joe and Ted took on the job of complying with the state's standards. It wasn't easy. They needed materials and blueprints and money and they had none of these things, but within 15 days, half the time the fire marshal had allowed, there were new clearly marked exit doors, new win-dows, fire detectors, fire extinguishers. I remember the pleased look on the marshal's face when he came back to inspect the work.

"Beautiful," he kept saying. "Yes, that will pass now." Then he let drop his final explosive. "Just be sure," he said, "that no more than five people live here at any one time. Otherwise it becomes a public housing facility and those clearances take years to get."

The visit from the fire marshal marked two changes at Love Inn. First I saw that I was no longer the sole head of the operation. Almost without realizing it—as most things happened at the farm—Joe and Ted had stepped in to assume that responsibility with me. And second, we were no longer a physical commune. People found rooms and apartments all around Ithaca. It was probably a healthy thing, keeping us from getting too ingrown and wrapped up in our own little world. But it caused problems, too, and the chief one was money.

Renting living quarters, eating in groups of two or three instead of all together, traveling to and from the barn, all of this cost more than we were earning. A number of us had paying jobs—as grocery clerks, farm hands, office help, construction workers—but even when these resources were pooled there wasn't enough to meet our personal expenses and keep the barn going as well.

Nedra and I weren't even getting the $125 a week the job at CBN used to bring in. The Scott Ross Show, which went out free to stations, cost more to produce than came in from donations.

And just at this point, when our need for money was most acute, the offerings habitually left by visitors in the Love Buckets at the barn suddenly and mysteriously dried up. Once, that summer of 1972, 20 of us lived for four days on twenty-five dollars. On the third day a visitor left a quarter in one of the Love Buckets. I carried that quarter in the palm of my hand all over the barn, showing people, rejoicing. If God was trying to teach us gratitude for everything we received, He was certainly succeeding.

All summer long the lean times continued. The odd thing was that the crowds at our music weekends and mid-week teaching sessions had never been greater. Just—the giving stopped. Our Volkswagen bus was still running fine, but we had no money for gasoline. We put ourselves on strict food rationing: no meat, eat only vegetables from the garden, buy day-old bread from the baker.

"One thing we know," Ted Sandquist pointed out, "there are

no accidents in God's Kingdom. He's allowing this for a reason."

And then one day Joe and I independently heard the same idea in our prayer time. The problem wasn't with other people's generosity; it was *we* who weren't giving enough. We'd always tithed all income at Love Inn, ten percent of all receipts going outside our own community. Now the incredible thought came that we were to double that amount.

If it hadn't been for the fact that we both got the same message on the same day, we might have ignored it. Here we were, just barely able to feed ourselves. But because of the coincidence we presented the idea to the whole group at the next family meeting, and to our amazement everyone agreed that it came from the Lord. So, we went ahead. Twenty percent. Off the top. Before any expenses were met. If a quarter appeared in the Love Bucket, we gave away a nickel.

And with this step came a remarkable change in our attitude about money. The *purpose* of income was different now. First and foremost we were to meet the needs of others. Part of the fun was giving in secret. The need could be right here at Ithaca: it might be a fund drive at a local school, or a neighbor who needed a vacation. Or it could be anywhere in the world. Biafra. Bangladesh.

And with the change also, suddenly, astonishingly, mysteriously, there was more money from which to take our double-tithe. Once again God provided, as He had in the beginning, in abundance beyond our dreams. We'd started publishing a newspaper at Love Inn, called *Free Love*. We knew we could save hundreds of dollars per issue in typesetting costs if we could buy a type-composing machine. But the machine cost $4,400. We'd raised part of this sum and were discussing where the rest was to come from, when Peg's quiet voice came from the back of the book room.

"I guess that's why the man settled up early."

A while back, Peg explained, she'd sold a building she owned in Ithaca, taking back a ten year mortgage. Peg had been receiving monthly checks from this note, but recently the new owner had decided to pay off the mortgage all at once. "His check just came in," said Peg. "I've been wondering what all that money was for . . ."

The Love Buckets, too, were suddenly overflowing. Donations poured in to the Scott Ross Show. They came from people who had visited the barn in the past. A note would arrive from Earmuff, Iowa. "Dear Scott. You don't remember me. But I came to Love Inn on an all-time high. You people there really helped me. Here's five bucks." Or from parents of young people we had helped, like the bald-headed fellow who stormed into Love Inn one night cursing us out and demanding to know "what the hell is going on here." I showed him around. At the end of the tour the man shoved a fistful of bills into my hand. "My daughter wasn't kidding then," was all he said. We never knew which of the girls who'd wandered into the barn was his daughter.

"Give, and it shall be given unto you; good measure, pressed down, and shaken together, and running over." These words from the Sermon on the Mount had sprung to life before our eyes.

And the more I thought about it, the more I realized that the whole thing had begun with that family meeting. I'd brought a financial decision to the group, and the group, together, had heard God's voice with more certainty than any individual among us could.

Why then was I still so reluctant to bring the whole of my life—oh, not to Jesus so much. That was comparatively easy: *He* understood, after all, *He* made allowances. What still terrified me was the thought of giving over the reins of my life to a group of human beings.

And then one day Joe said something that was like a light going on in a dark corner. He'd just come back from a trip to visit one of our "offspring" groups, communities started by people who'd had their training at Love Inn. It was a trip the whole community had prayed about, decided upon, sent Joe off on. "And it's the first time," he said, "I've ever taken a trip where I haven't expected something terrible to happen. A plane crash, an automobile accident—it's crazy, but I've always had these morbid fears when I've travelled."

Morbid fear . . . I thought of the irrational, senseless terror that could still grip me in the course of an ordinary stroll down the street.

I found myself remembering something else. The nightly bombing raids over Glasgow. Certainly I'd been in more real danger then than I'd ever been in since. And yet—I hadn't known what fear was. Was it, I suddenly wondered, because as a small child I'd been, humbly and unquestioningly, un 'er the authority of flesh and blood representatives of God? "Covered" by my father and mother, in the Christian phrase? Was it this covering Joe had experienced on his trip?

With Joe's example I began to share—just with him and Ted at first—my own fears, to talk about these secret areas of my life. I told them about the pizza oven, and the rubbery buildings, and the snipers on the rooftops. All the silly child's-nightmare things, and my own role in opening up my psyche and spirit to such phantoms. I told them about the visitations from the dazzling "angel of light" and the paralyzing terror that had come with them.

The relief I felt as I stammered out each confession was more than just getting it out into the open. Even as it happened I knew that somehow, in bringing it to these visible, physical members of His Body, I was bringing it to Jesus Himself in a whole new way, and that His power was setting me free.

I was learning to submit my fears to the Body of Christ, and I was getting free of them. But . . . what about my lusts? My resentments? What about the sex fantasy I'd wallowed in all last week? The way I'd exploded at Nedra when she wasn't ready on time? No, there were certain things I knew I'd never be able to share with anyone . . .

One day Jacki brought the morning mail over to Peg's house and sat down to wait while I thumbed through it.

"What's this?" I asked, holding up a phonograph record. Jacki didn't know. The record had simply appeared, along with a note, handwritten and brief:

"The guy who plays guitar here is a Christian from Youngstown, Ohio."

Later, I put it on. It was by a group called the Glass Harp and from the label I saw that the lead guitarist was a guy named Phil Keaggy. I put the needle down and listened to the most incredible sound. Keaggy was unreal. He could do things with a guitar that weren't in the instrument.

But—what did it have to do with us? I put the record away, and forgot it.

That fall, 1972, a thought kept coming during my morning time: we were supposed to become involved at Love Inn in recorded music. Repeatedly, I dismissed the idea. It would cost a fortune, and besides, it would take a huge staff. It was true, some incredibly talented people had recently been led to the community—Eleanor Smith, Peter Hopper, Gary and Mary Hamilton, Mutt and Ann Minton, John and Nancy Shorey, Duane McNett, Pierre and Maggie Joseph. Still, we already had much too much to do.

The Scott Ross Show, for example. We were now sending tapes to 80 stations, and it was long past the time when we needed our own studio. We decided as a group—at least where Love Inn affairs were concerned I no longer even attempted the solo act—that the studio should be built under the eaves at the barn, raising the roof in one place to make room for it. We set out to pray in the money.

Like the check from Mia Hansen which showed we were on the right track to order food in bulk, money simply appeared. It flooded us from everywhere at once, as it had never come before. Pat Robertson helped us. So did Nedra's mother. Noel Stookey heard about what we were doing and joined in. Old friends from New York wrote, sending money. The show itself stimulated giving. Even our neighbors and area farmers wanted to be a part of the new project. In all more than $20,000 came in.

That would equip quite a studio! Surely we didn't need such a fancy facility just for the Scott Ross Show. Perhaps our thinking had not been big enough?

I was wrestling with this one morning when Jacki buzzed me for a long distance call. I picked up the receiver.

"This is Phil Keaggy."

My mind drew a blank. And then I remembered: the uncanny lead guitarist from Youngstown, Ohio. "I got this strong impression last night that I was supposed to call you," Phil Keaggy said. "Got anything going on?"

"I can't believe this . . ." I said, and then I told Keaggy about the brand new studio and the idea we'd discussed at a family meeting the previous evening for recording top-quality Jesus music under a label called New Song Productions. Phil caught the idea right away. We'd put an album together. We'd keep costs down because he would do the whole session himself, overdubbing the various instruments.

So it was that toward the end of 1972 Phil Keaggy came to Love Inn. There was one surprise right off the bat. When he was a boy Phil had gotten his right hand mangled in an old-fashioned farm pump. Phil Keaggy produced his unbelievable music with only nine fingers.

The owner of our apartment on Elm Street had decided to remodel the building and once more Nedra and I were looking for a place to live. Joe and Ted were both married now. Joe and his wife Ann had moved to West Groton. Ted and Dawn had found a rental nearby. Nedra and I decided to build a log house of our own on the Love Inn property. The day we sunk a shovel into the rocky upstate soil we also purchased a third-hand mobile home to live in until the house was ready. We parked it in the field back of Peg's.

"It's full circle, Scott," said Nedra. Shouted, rather: Nedra Kristina (an Indian chief) was chasing Christian Scott (paleface settler, still wearing diapers) around the small formica table, with war whoops which demonstrated there was nothing the matter nowadays with her bronchial tubes. "We're back in a Tin Can again."

And it was in Tin Can Two that the struggle continued over what I still considered "mine" as opposed to "His"—or worse yet, "theirs." Once it was an ad for an x-rated movie which caught my eye. I let my mind play with the provocative title, spinning out the story as I imagined it to be. There was a hill across Route 13 from the barn where I often went when I wanted to be alone. I went up there now, and it was there that the Lord showed me how easy it is to say "I lay down my life." What was hard to give up were the little pamperings, the private areas where we indulged ourselves. "You think you have a right to these things because they're inside your own mind. Don't you know yet that you have no 'right' to anything? As long as you have rights, you have not really laid down your life."

I remember walking for a long time on that hillside that day. I remember kicking the trees.

All during the fall and winter of '73–'74, the Lord reminded me in a hundred ways that a Christian has no "rights." Now that we lived next to the barn, I had no right to sleep through the night, no right to avoid being waked at four in the morning to talk to a runaway, or fix him a bowl of soup. I had no right to a car of my own. These things were sometimes granted me by the grace of God, but never as "rights."

Above all I had no right to keep part of my life hidden. I had no privilege the Lord didn't have as He hung naked before the world on the cross.

But you know, God talks only so long to someone with his fingers in his ears. Suddenly the communication seemed to cease. My prayers stopped getting answers. Clouds of darkness hung over me. I was brusque with Jacki and Peg, Ted and Joe, Nedra and the kids . . . everyone. During our Tuesday night teaching sessions I had nothing to say. Everyone knew I was going through a heavy time. One cold February afternoon Ted came into my office and found me sitting on the sofa, in tears.

"I don't know what's hurting you, Scott," Ted said, "but I'll go through it with you."

"Yeah. Thanks, Ted."

I couldn't say to him how much those words meant. They were

to mean even more as the Lord began to peel back the layers of my heart, revealing what was really there.

It was a Sunday morning in March. Nedra Kristina had already run up to the barn where the worship service would soon be starting. Nedra, who was pregnant again, was sitting with me at the formica table in the kitchen of the trailer, putting off the moment when it would be time to clear away the breakfast dishes. Two-year-old Christian was puddling with his orange juice. I told him to stop, but he continued to pour the juice out of his cup.

"Christian!" I shouted. I slammed my hand on the table. The little boy looked up, startled. *"Stop that!"*

"Now Scott," said Nedra. Her voice was soothing. "Aren't you overreacting?"

"What do you mean?" I shouted again, my voice bouncing off the metal walls.

"You're terribly angry, honey."

"I'm not angry!" I yelled, furious.

And then the most amazing thing happened. I reached down and grabbed the edge of the table where we were sitting and yanked it upward. The dishes, the juice, the coffee, all went flying. Nedra jumped up. Christian stared at me from his highchair.

Nedra picked up the telephone.

I reached over and tore it out of her hands. Then I tried to yank the whole instrument out of the wall.

Nedra waited a while, frozen. Then very softly she said. "This is it. This is really it, Mr. Scott Ross."

I ran into the little bedroom. In a moment I heard the front door softly close. I waited, then crept out again. The dining room was empty, a shambles. The table was upside down. Juice and oatmeal and marmalade ran together on the linoleum. I started to cry as I picked up the pieces of broken glass.

"It's no good Lord. It's just no good at all."

I expected someone to come down. But an hour passed and there was no knock on the door. Finally I walked slowly up to the barn. I could hear the service going on up in the loft. I went to the kitchen and made myself a cup of tea. Pierre Joseph looked in, rubbing his black mustache.

"How are you doing, Scott?"

"Ask me no questions I'll tell you no lies."

Pierre and his wife were relative newcomers to the barn, but he was a perceptive guy. "We'll stick by you, Scott. Through anything."

After the service I locked myself in my office with Ted and Joe.

I described the ugly scene at the breakfast table, blow-by-shard-by-tear. They did not condemn me; they did not excuse me. They heard me out, and then again that mysterious phenomenon of oneness in Christ occurred: they shouldered the experience with me. With me and for me they lifted it to Jesus; with Him and for Him they spoke words of forgiveness I could never have believed if I had heard them only with an inner ear. Then they went with me down to the trailer and stood by while I apologized to Nedra and asked her forgiveness.

And with, and in spite of, and through the pain, I could sense God at work. He was using this experience to show me what was in my heart. Murder. A rage quite out of my control. Something that had been inside of me since—I tried to remember how long.

I recalled the anger I had felt toward the soot-stained church on the drab Glasgow street, the church that wouldn't let me play soccer on Sunday with the other kids. I remembered the bullies I'd encountered when I first came to America. The homosexual who made a pass at me in my bedroom. I remembered the hypocrites, the backbiters, the man in the big New York church who turned me away because I didn't have on the right clothes, the listener in Portsmouth who was going to shoot me because I had prayed for dying Martin Luther King.

And suddenly I saw that in every case I'd been telling myself I had a "right" to be angry.

But . . . if I had no rights, then that included anger too—no matter how "justified." I had to give it up, every bit of it, and not just to my own private concept of God, but to Christ as He existed here and now in flesh and blood people.

It took quite a while, unloading the resentments one by one to Joe and Ted, but as I did, healing began. Deep, lasting healing. The red brick church-on-the-corner, for example, that I'd held in such contempt so long. Bit by bit with the help of the others I uncovered the roots of this ugly plant—a hurt here, a disillusionment there— and saw how I'd let these few experiences spread to choke off my relationship with millions of my fellow Christians.

To see it, to confess it, to repent of it—I don't know whether I could ever have done these things shut away in a private prayer closet somewhere. Above all, to know finally that I was forgiven, and to start again. Already, in fact for years, Love Inners without my hang-ups had been quietly serving churches all over the area. Preaching on Sundays, transporting the elderly, helping with their youth programs. When I began to join them it was as though walls which had kept my ministry shut up in a narrow channel tumbled down, and a whole world of service, of speaking, of fellowship opened up.

I remember the family meeting when I knew it was really happening. We were discussing where 20% of a recent donation to Love Inn should go, when someone remembered a nearby church which was badly in need of new seats. We agreed on this and had gone on to other matters before I realized that the church in fact was located on a corner, and that the person making the suggestion had been me.

The hardest healing of all, however, lay ahead.

The date was April 4th, 1974. A group of us from Love Inn had gone over to the local high school gym as we did every week, to play basketball. Once more that black cloud engulfed me. I was sick of basketball. I was sick of the whole stupid scene at Love Inn. Finally I just walked off the court.

"Aren't you going to play any more, Scott?"

"No."

I went to the locker room, showered, got in my car and roared away. In spite of the gas shortage I took off on a long trek over the back country roads. It didn't help. Returning to Ithaca I drove to Pierre Joseph's house and knocked on his door.

"I'm going to get drunk," I said. "Will you come with me?"

Pierre looked at me. But he said nothing and shortly we were sitting on stools at a local bar and I was downing beers as fast as I could. It reminded me of New York when I would handle my uptightness with alcohol. Only—tonight for some reason I couldn't get high.

After an hour I got worrying about Nedra and went to the pay phone to call her. "Where are you, Scott?" Nedra asked. I told her. "What's happening, honey?" she said.

"I wish I knew."

A girl came into the bar and sat down on a stool.

"Dawn Sandquist's here with me," said Nedra. "We're praying for you." I didn't want to hear about it. I told Nedra I wanted out of Love Inn. I just wanted to do my own thing, whatever that was. I wanted to be *free*.

The girl shifted on her stool, and I caught a glimpse of a tremendous figure silhouetted against the row of illuminated liquor bottles behind the bar.

I said goodbye to Nedra and went back to my stool. Pierre wanted to call his wife too and left me alone with the girl. I found myself wondering why Pierre had come, since he obviously wasn't in a party mood. "We'll stick by you," he'd told me. Words from a psalm dropped into my mind: *Though I make my bed in hell, thou art there . . .*

Pierre took a long time. While he was away I struck up a conversation with the girl. Soon we were sitting closer to each other.

"How're things at home?" I asked as Pierre appeared again.

Pierre shrugged.

"Maybe you'd better be with Maggie," I said. "I'll be all right."

Pierre sat down on the stool, making no move to leave.

"I mean it, Pierre." I didn't say the words *get lost* but that was the message, and it must have been clear, for Pierre said, ":All right,

Scott," and got up. As he was leaving he looked me straight in the eye: "It's now, Scott, isn't it?" What a strange remark. What's "now"?

As soon as he closed the door I turned back to the girl.

"Your friend doesn't seem very happy," she said.

"He's Lebanese."

"What's that got to do with it?"

"When you see things through Arabian eyes they look upside down."

The girl looked at me quizzically. It was like I was tripping again. An hour passed on the Four Roses clock on the wall. The girl put her hand on my arm and asked for another drink. When it came she didn't take her hand away. And suddenly I knew for sure that in addition to the sin of murder, I was also capable of adultery.

We were the only two left in the place and the bartender kept looking at his watch. Finally he said it outright. Closing time. As I paid the bill I knew that I was at the crossroad. I watched the girl get down off her barstool. The words I said next would chart our course. It was like Pierre said. The time was now. I took a breath . . .

"At-Love-Inn-we-help-people-find-the-Lord." The words came out in a rush.

The girl stopped still. She stared into my face as though she couldn't have heard right. And as she did I remembered the time I'd torn a ligament in my leg as we were getting siding from a neighbor's barn to build the new studio. The pain was so bad I was afraid I was going to faint. And then I made a discovery. I could bear the pain if I talked about Jesus.

This moment of temptation was like pain. It gripped like pain. It forced all the attention on itself, as pain does.

"Because we've found that Jesus is the answer to every problem. He can help us even when we can't help ourselves."

And suddenly I saw the humor in the situation. Here I was walking out the door of a bar with a girl who had made it clear she was interested, and I'm talking about Jesus! We both began to laugh so hard from the pent-up tension that the bartender, following us, snapping out lights, turned to stare.

"You all right?" he said.

"Yes." I spoke with feeling. "Yes, I'm all right."

The girl drove me to Love Inn since Pierre had taken the car. She let me out at the top of the driveway.

"I can't figure you," she said as she put the motor in reverse. "But, well, thanks for what you said—about finding answers and everything."

I took my time walking down the hill. The sky was already turning pale. Inside the trailer Nedra was asleep. I picked up the telephone and dialed Ted Sandquist. The phone rang only once.

"Can you come down?"

Within ten minutes Ted knocked on the door. We walked together in the early dawn light through the wet pasture down to the pond. We just talked. Later guys came to the nearly finished log house and started working on the roof. I guessed from the way they kept staring at us, they knew something was going on.

I spewed out everything to Ted. I told him about the girl and the adultery I'd seen in my heart.

Ted had just one question. "Have you repented, Scott?"

I didn't answer that right away. I wanted to be sure about it. Then I said,

"Yes, Ted. I have repented. I made my decision when I headed back here. I want to turn it all over, every grubby corner of it, to the Lord and to the people here."

Together we went back to the Tin Can. Nedra was holding Christian in her lap. I stood looking down into her incredible eyes.

"Is it all right, Scott?"

How could I say it was all right. I began to sob.

"Are these dramas going to keep happening?" Nedra asked. "I couldn't take that."

But somehow I knew they were not going to keep happening. Healing, effective, permanent healing, was taking place. Not through any decision of mine to shape up, but because of the Body of Christ. I'd had a hint of the Body's strength years ago, down in

Portsmouth, when some people at CBN formed a circle around me in a hallway, and an enemy I'd struggled with endlessly as a single individual, simply took to his heels at the united voice of the church.

I'd been too scared then to grasp what had happened, too busy running toward where I thought freedom was. I wasn't running any more.

All this was almost two years ago now. Since that April night I've had some flare-ups of temper, and being human I have been tempted. Whenever this happens my old enemy, so adept at dressing himself up in light, whispers, "See, you haven't changed at all." But that's just not true. When I yielded my "rights" to anger and desire to the Body of Christ, they really did lose their power. And when ghosts of the past rise up, I know where to turn to get the victory.

I remember a while back we were getting ready for a concert at one of the local colleges. The guy who was supposed to set up the amplifying equipment arrived late and there was a big crisis. "Why can't you ever get anything straight!" I exploded at him, and strode off the stage.

I got two strides away, that is. Then two strides back. Apologize for my rudeness, and ask everybody on the stage to pray that I'd be able to master my temper. In 45 seconds a situation that could once have seethed for hours or days, destroying harmony, disrupting relationships, was confessed, healed, finished.

Victory! That's the theme-song of the church. Not just over the darkness in our lives, but in the work God gives us to do. Healing, for example. What He couldn't trust me to do as a single individual, He allows me to witness as part of a group. Bill and Peg Nichols, who gave us the red-and-white Volkswagen, have a son, Lynn, who with his wife Kathy is now a member of the community. Lynn and Kathy's baby was born with a dislocated hip. Just before she was to undergo surgery we prayed for her and that hip was instantaneously healed. Jim and Debbie Harrington were told they could not have children. We prayed for them and now Debbie is expecting her second baby. Jim had to wear thick glasses until we prayed for his eyes to be healed. Now he runs the farm with no glasses at all. I myself have had an unusual healing—of my teeth of all things. There are before-and-after X rays to verify arrest of two cavities and the "disappearance" of five more. Recently a dentist studied the X rays. "That's God," was his only comment.

Or ministry. Ours is far greater than any Lone Ranger could achieve. Recently we opened a grade school at the barn, headed by a Spirit-anointed teacher, Ragnhild Kjeldaas. The radio show goes out over 150 stations. Between that and *Free Love* Jacki and her staff answer more than 600 letters a week.

Victory in everyday problems. There are 250 of us in the Love Inn community now—two are Nedra's mother and my Mum— and every one of us has some daily experience of His power. Just keeping the books now is a complicated job involving 27 different postings under five categories—Love Inn, New Song Productions, the bookshop, *Free Love,* and the Scott Ross Show. The possibilities for mix-ups are enormous. Peg Hardesty and our young business manager, John Shorey, start working on the books a little after nine o'clock every Monday morning. They pray before they start, they pray for each other as they work. By five in the evening they are ready to see if God has once again done the impossible. John's finger poises over the calculator key. He punches it. Time after time the endless long columns balance to the penny!

The other day I climbed to the top of the hill opposite the barn and sat looking over the farm and thinking about all the victory going on down there. I could see our snug log cabin house where our second little girl, Heather Brooke Ross, is just learning to walk. And the silo with its new colored glass dome, where 24 hours a day prayer goes up for our needs and the ones we hear about.

I could see Peg Hardesty and Ted Sandquist standing in the parking lot with a carload of new arrivals. Peg is positively skinny today after losing 45 pounds for the Lord. It was too far away to see her face but I knew for sure she was smiling.

That's the church down there, I thought suddenly. The church that I feared and fled for so many years, while I looked for freedom in every other place.

And then I'd made a discovery. The church—that's just another name for Jesus. Not Jesus the historical figure, or Jesus the invisible Spirit (though He's both of those too, of course.) But Jesus in bodily form on earth.

I saw Nedra come out of our house with Heather in her arms. And suddenly I knew there was only one place in the world I wanted to be. Only one girl in the world I wanted to share it all with. Jesus had set me free at last to be myself. I ran through the hummocks of grass down the hill to home.